W9-BGF-432

ISLE

ROYALE

Superior Wilderness

NATIONAL

PARK

Superior Wilderness

ISLE ROYALE NATIONAL PARK

by
Napier Shelton

ISLE ROYALE NATURAL HISTORY ASSOCIATION
HOUGHTON, MICHIGAN

Copyright 1997 by the Isle Royale Natural History Association,
Houghton Michigan

ISBN 0-935289-09-7

Library of Congress Catalog Card Number 97-76804

Book Design by Christina Watkins
Project Management by Jill Burkland and Robert Linn
Map art, pages 8–9, by Michael Hyslop, Michigan Technological
    University
Illustration, page 40, by Stephen D. Veirs, Jr.
Typography and Production by Penny Smith, TypeWorks
Lithography by Courier Graphics, Inc., Phoenix, Arizona

Photography Credits:

Tom Bean — cover inset, aspen.

George H. H. Huey — page 57.

Robert Johnsonn — pages 5 (bottom), 15, 18, 23, 26 (both), 59, 60 (both),
61 (both), 63, 76, 80, 104, 105, 106 (bottom), 111, 122, 137, 152 (both).

John and Ann Mahan — cover insets: gull, wolf, berries; pages 1, 2, 45,
48, 50, 65 (both), 84, 90, 91 (top), 106 (top), 107, 109, 114, 115, 131,
136, 150, 155, 159 (both), 165, 175, 176.

National Park Service — cover background; pages 13, 22, 27 (right), 33,
34, 36, 53, 54, 55, 69, 87, 88, 91 (bottom), 95, 120, 127, 135, 142, 151,
156, 161, 167.

Rolf O. Peterson — pages 117, 147.

Scot Stewart — pages 5 (top), 27 (left), 73 (right), 83, 99, 108, 128, 132,
133.

Contents

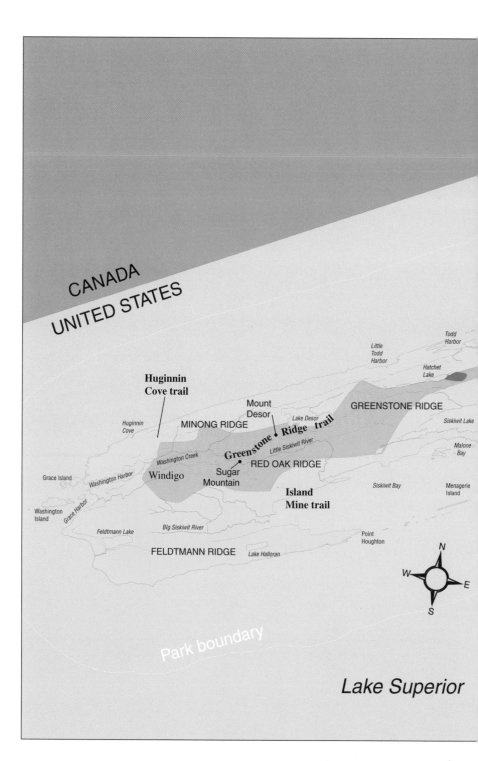

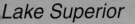
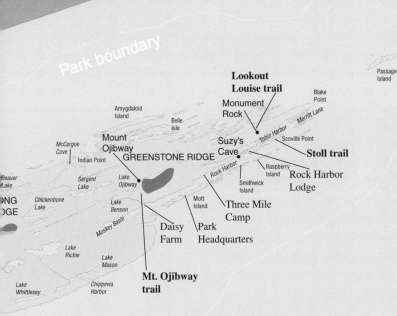
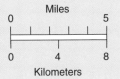

Preface

*T*his book is a natural history of Isle Royale for the layman, although I hope it will interest scientists as well. It emphasizes the ecology of the island and surrounding waters—that is, the relationships among their plants, animals, and physical environments. The human history has been viewed largely from the standpoint of its impact on the land and water. The book has been written in a way that I hope will benefit armchair travelers as well as those fortunate people who actually visit the island.

Superior Wilderness is an extensive revision of my earlier work, *The Life of Isle Royale*, published by the National Park Service in 1975. New information has been added mostly in sidebars and the chapters "Lake Superior" and "The Guardians"; and changes on the island since the 1970s have been described. These changes include dramatic fluctuations in wolf and moose populations, a noticeable increase of otters, and an explosion of cormorants, as well as more subtle changes in the forests.

Superintendent Douglas Barnard and his staff, especially Terry Lindsay, were most helpful in providing information, lodging, and transportation around the island. Researchers Ted Gostomski, Emmet Judziewicz, Robert Janke, Rolf Peterson, Richard Schorfhaar, Gary Curtis, and Mary

Curtis kindly shared their specialized knowledge. Reviewers of the manuscript included Terry Lindsay and other members of the park staff, Robert Linn and Gayle Pekkala of the Isle Royale Natural History Association, Robert Janke, Rolf Peterson, William Rose, and Patrick Martin of Michigan Technological University, and Richard Schorfhaar, director of the Marquette Fisheries Station, who reviewed sections on Lake Superior and fish.

Bob Linn has shepherded me through this entire project, even transporting me to various locations in his small craft when the trip was uncomfortably bumpy. I extend him special thanks. I would also like to thank the Isle Royale Natural History Association, which arranged transport for me on the *Ranger III* and handled the many challenges of book publication.

Since much of the text of *The Life of Isle Royale* remains in this book, I thank again the people who assisted me with that work, especially Robert Janke, Rolf Peterson, Durward Allen, D. B. Botkin, Peter Jordan, N. King Huber, H. E. Wright, Robert Johnsson, and the staff of the park at that time, especially Superintendent Hugh Beattie, Alan Eliason, and Frank Deckert.

All of the above, added to the earlier students of Isle Royale whom I read, laid the foundation for this book.

N.S.

Arrival

"*T*here it is!" someone exclaims. Rousing from a half-sleep, we part the curtains and look north across the wide gray waters of Lake Superior. Along the horizon floats a thin, dark strip—indistinct, almost a part of the water. From this point, halfway across the world's greatest lake in the lounge of the gently rolling *Ranger III*, Isle Royale is pure mystery.

We doze occasionally, and each time we awaken, that thin line has stretched and widened. Finally we join the growing group on the deck. Like everyone else, we wonder what that remote island is like and what it holds in store for us.

As the vessel approaches Middle Islands Passage, the island begins to reveal itself. We see long outcroppings of gray rock. We see thick forest, pale green with birches and dark with the spires of spruce and fir. Across the water drifts the faint pungency of those firs, saying, as nothing else can, "North Woods." Entering Rock Harbor, we see the dark rocks along the shore, taking the lake's pounding below and wearing a band of orange lichens above the waves' reach. Herring gulls wheel against the backdrop of forest, rock, and sky. Ducks and cormorants patter away at the vessel's approach.

But there are few clues to what is happening on this great forested rock—the unfolding of petals under the trees, the burgeoning of young life, the deadly game between predator and prey. And there is hardly a hint about what it will be like to live on this wild island for the next small part of our lives.

To step onto Isle Royale is to leave behind one's old self and one's old world and to begin a new exploration into the nature of life.

Mott Island materializes in early morning mist.

We Walk on the Past

*E*arly in our visit to Isle Royale we set out to climb up through the enclosing forests to a ridgetop, from where we can see the lay of this island and try to grasp it whole. After making camp at Daisy Farm on Rock Harbor, we start up the Mt. Ojibway Trail. Spruces, firs, and birches rise above us. For a little stretch our feet slip on rounded stones. Up the south side of Ransom Hill, where the forest opens and the trail steepens, we breathe a bit harder. Down the hill's more abrupt north side, where the white columns of paper birch surround us, we apply the brakes a bit. Now our boots thump on the simple bridge across Tobin Creek, which has been widened and deepened by a dam built by beavers somewhere downstream. Then up and over another hill, across a small swamp near Lake Ojibway, and a longer climb toward Mt. Ojibway, a promontory of Greenstone Ridge. The forest thins, clumps of small maples appear, and as we gain the smooth-rocked shrubby top of Mt. Ojibway and ascend the fire tower, the island opens before us.

We see a strikingly striated pattern of land and water — elongated, parallel forms that might have been created by a giant comb raking the emergent rocks in a northeast-south-west direction. Parallel ridges, dominated by the island's backbone — Greenstone Ridge — state the theme most boldly.

Where the ridges reach Lake Superior they continue underwater, sometimes emerging to form narrow islands. The long, linear troughs between ridges here and there hold a stretched-out lake; and where the valleys reach the big lake they form long, deep coves.

Plant distribution accentuates this parallel pattern. Light green aspen and birch dominate many ridges, while dark green coniferous forests lie in the troughs. Stretching along some ridgetops are open strips of grass and shrubs, through which the underlying rock mass often outcrops. Fifteen miles to the north, the mesa-like shapes of Thunder Cape rise along the Canadian shore, close to but irrevocably separated from the island by the cold, plunging depths of Lake Superior.

The Amygdaloid Island region of the park strikingly displays the ridge-and-trough topography of the archipelago.

All of it—the hills we sweatingly crossed, the forest scenes we glimpsed, the overall pattern itself—is the legacy of past events. The varying composition of the forest has been dictated by the topography, shaped slowly over eons by forgotten fires, by storms of yesteryear, by centuries of animal activity, and by a thousand little colonizations and extinctions during the island's history. The stones we slipped on near the start of our hike lie on an ancient beach formed by an ancestor of Lake Superior. The island's lakes owe their existence to great, gouging glaciers that thawed only a tick of geological time ago. And our legs ache today because the processes that formed and eroded the rocks millions of years ago created a corrugated topography.

The surface scene that spreads before us—lakes, forests, and the life-giving soil—is the work of 11,000 years, a very short time by nature's standards. During those 110 centuries the island appeared from beneath glacial ice; rose as the lake level dropped; was colonized by plants and animals; developed a little soil and a heavy, ever-changing forest; and experienced the beginning and inevitable shrinking of its many inland lakes.

Yet the creation of the rocks and the development of their ridge-and-trough pattern are the work of millions of years—a span of time in which the formation of Lake Superior and its islands is only the most recent event. Isle Royale's rocks date from the formation of the Superior Basin, an episode that was to shape all subsequent geologic events in the region.

Some 1.2 billion years ago, the earth's crust cracked along a great rift zone that stretched through the middle of the area now occupied by Lake Superior and may have bent southward toward the present Gulf of Mexico. Through this series of cracks poured molten lava, forced up by pressures deep within the earth. A hundred times or more, flaming sheets flowed out from the fissures, eventually covering thousands of square miles. As they did, the land along the rift zone sank, forming a basin.

Some of the lava flows, like the Greenstone Flow that underlies Isle Royale's main ridge, are among the largest and thickest found anywhere on earth. The lavas ponded in the Lake Superior Basin, forming a great magma ocean, which took tens to hundreds of years to solidify. The great columns of the Palisades and Monument Rock, at the north end of the island, reflect this long solid-ification process.

In the quiet periods be-tween flows, rock material was washed from the rim of this great basin toward its center. After the last erup-tion, streams continued to carry boulders, pebbles, sand grains, and fine silt from the rim hills down toward the still-sinking basin plains. These events left a rock rec-ord consisting, beneath, of thick layers of volcanic rock alternating with thin layers of sandstone and conglom-erate (composed of rounded rock fragments cemented to-gether by finer material). On top of those layers are sev-eral thousand more feet of sandstone and conglomerate. These rocks—volcanic, sand-stone, and conglomerate—form the bedrock of Isle Royale, with the volcanic basalt predominant on most of the island and the reddish sedimentary rock forming the surface in the Feldtmann Ridge-Big Siskiwit River

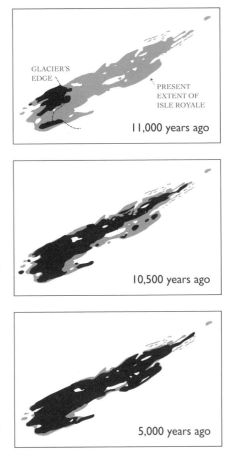

GLACIER'S EDGE

PRESENT EXTENT OF ISLE ROYALE

11,000 years ago

10,500 years ago

5,000 years ago

Since the last glaciation, Isle Royale has gradually been emerging from lake waters as the land rebounds from its depressed state under glacial ice and the ancestral Great Lakes cut successively lower outlets. At the rate of a foot or more per century, the land continues to rise today.

area. The arrangement of these rocks in layers and their differing resistance to erosion dictated the island's present ridge-and-valley topography.

About 30 million years after the lava flows cooled, faulting—displacement along a crack in the earth's crust—occurred, thrusting some sections of it upward and adjacent sections downward. One of these faults ran along what is now the center of the Keweenaw Peninsula, on the Michigan shore. Another is thought to have opened along the north edge of Isle Royale, which would account for the present projection of this piece of land above Lake Superior. Lesser faults cracked across the island, forming such depressions as McCargoe Cove and the valley that is followed by a section of the Huginnin Cove Trail.

McCargoe Cove occupies a depression formed by a diagonal fault in the northeast part of Isle Royale.

Coincident with the faulting, pressures in the earth forced hot, mineral-bearing solutions up into the cavities and cracks in the rock. One of the minerals thus deposited was copper. Occurring in its pure, or "native" state, the veins and masses of copper lay within the rock until the far-distant time when people would come hunting it. Those who walk the island's narrow pebble beaches today can see other minerals—such as quartz; white, red, or yellow heulandite; white or yellow stilbite; and banded agate—which filled gas bubbles within the basalt and eventually were broken free by the pounding waves.

Between the deposition of Isle Royale's uppermost conglomerate and the work of the most recent glacier there is an enormous gap in the geologic record. Whatever deposits were laid down during those millions of years were subsequently eroded away, leaving the layers we have described to form the land's surface. Depressed in the center of the Superior Basin, these layers rose toward the basin's rim, where their edges were exposed in parallel bands. The bands of sandstone and conglomerate, being less resistant than the volcanic basalt, eroded faster. Streams tended to flow along the depressions started in these more vulnerable rocks, gradually deepening them. In this way, Isle Royale's bands of basalt remained higher to form ridges, while valleys developed on the sandstone and conglomerate between them. The south slopes of ridges remained fairly gentle, following the dip of the layers toward the center of the basin, while north slopes—the eroded edges of layers—dropped off steeply.

This pattern was accentuated and somewhat modified by the series of glaciers that rode down over the northern United States during the last million years. A cooling trend, accompanied perhaps by greater precipitation, produced more snow across Canada during the winters than could be melted during the summers. As the snow accumulated, it was compressed into ice; and under pressure of the growing mass it finally began to move. Four major advances of these continental glaciers, separated by long intervals of mild climate during which the ice sheets melted, scoured the land as far south as the Ohio River. A large river valley is thought to have occupied the center of the Superior Basin during the glacial period and to have channeled the immensely thick lobes of ice flowing through that area. The last major glaciation, known as the Wisconsinan, ended in the Superior area

Four major advances of continental glaciers scoured this region as far south as the present-day Ohio River. Illustrated here are the Pleistocene Ice sheets.

only a few thousand years ago, leaving behind the ancestral Great Lakes, thousands of smaller lakes, and deposits of rock debris the glacier had scraped up and pulverized in its crushing advance.

Today on Isle Royale we can see many places where the ice, perhaps a mile thick, smoothed and rounded the rock, and other places where, pushing boulders over the bedrock, it carved long grooves. Running generally northeast-southwest, these grooves indicate that the glaciers moved mostly parallel to the ridges. Scouring the valleys deeper, the ice made depressions where lakes formed after its retreat. On the southwestern part of the island, where the last glacier paused in its retreat, are small, linear hills made of its deposits.

The dying of the last glacier led to the birth of modern Isle Royale. As it melted northward across the Superior Basin, which it had scoured and depressed, the ice formed a gigantic dam for its own meltwater, thus creating the first ancestor of Lake Superior. About 11,000 years ago, the ice front lay across the southwest end of that section of land we now call Isle Royale, leaving three-fourths of it buried under ice and the southwest quarter partly above and partly beneath the water. The shoreline then stood at about the present 800-foot contour. After a long pause at this position, the ice resumed its rapid retreat northward, leaving a thin mantle of deposits on the southwest end, where melting had been very slow, but very little material on the central and northeast sections, where melting had been rapid.

What did our island look like, newly relieved of its ice burden some 10,800 years ago? Studies by geologist N. King Huber indicate that about half of present-day Isle Royale projected above the water. Much of the southwest end was in one piece, but the northeast end tailed off to a long, thin peninsula flanked by island chains. Glacial till of sand, silt, and stones softened the contours on the southwest part and covered most of the bedrock, but toward the northeast most of the rock was exposed.

Like earth before primeval life, Isle Royale stood barren, waiting.

Life Comes to the Island

*A*t the time of Isle Royale's birth, many forms of life were pressing northward as the warming climate rapidly destroyed the ice and exposed the land. Which ones first crossed the water to those smooth gray rocks, pounded by frigid waves, and to those bare, sandy hills?

Then as now, the wind and water carried spores and

Lichens, among the first plants to become established in a new, rocky environment, help prepare the way for mosses, ferns, and eventually flowering plants.

fragments of algae, mosses, and lichens, and some of these undoubtedly settled on the new surface. Algae gained a foothold in wet places, and the mosses and lichens pioneered mostly on rock, wet or dry. The air, the lake waves, and perhaps also wandering birds carried seeds of higher plants from the forests and grasslands south of the ice border. Some of these seeds—those from plants best adapted to cold, sterile conditions—germinated and grew on thin glacial deposits or in cracks in the rock, now beginning to collect soil particles.

Quite likely, many of the early colonists were tundra plants, of species now found only in the Arctic or on high mountains. Gradually these grasses, sedges, dwarf birches and willows, and other low-growing plants wove a green carpet over the gray-brown hills, except in the many places where rock still resisted. Perhaps here and there, in sheltered spots, spruce trees grew.

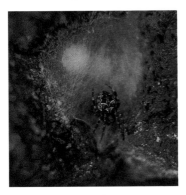

Spiders, by virtue of their abundance and variety, have important roles as predators in most terrestrial communities.

Where there is plant food, animals can follow, and no doubt the vanguard was not long in coming. Airborne insects and microscopic animals drifting down upon the greening landscape now could survive. Birds could begin nesting here. A few caribou may have arrived across the lake's winter ice. Close on the heels of the plant eaters came animals that preyed on them, including insects, spiders, hawks, and owls. If there were caribou, wolves may well have braved the 15-mile ice crossing to hunt them.

On the Isle Royale of 10,500 years ago, we can imagine a scene much like that of the Subarctic today. Mats of grasses and bright flowering little plants cover the ridgetops; shrubby birches and willows fill the draws; and down in the wet valleys scattered spruces raise their dark spires. Small bands of caribou, pausing frequently to scan the landscape for wolves, move up the hillside, browsing shrubs and nipping ground plants. But this is a transitory scene in the story of Isle Royale, for the forest is coming.

As the ice retreated, the land, relieved of its great burden, slowly rose. The basin's waters, also lifted somewhat by the rising land beneath, flowed out through the lowest available outlet. Over the centuries, the trend was for land areas to rise higher above the water level, as downcutting and escape through successively lower outlets generally resulted in lowering the elevation of the water surface.

By about 10,500 B.P. (years before present), the glacial ice had receded to the northern edge of the Superior Basin, which was then occupied by Lake Minong. This lake, which emptied by way of the Au Train-Whitefish Strait (Munising, Michigan, area) and St. Marys Strait (Sault Ste. Marie area), remained stable for many years, thus building well-defined shorelines that are easily traced today. On Isle Royale, Lake Minong shore features are found at elevations of about 680 to 765 feet above sea level. (Subsequent uneven uplift accounts for the present-day elevation of 600 feet above sea level.) These features include beach ridges (just west of Siskiwit Bay one is followed by the Feldtmann Ridge Trail) and numerous examples of lake erosion of the lava flows, such as sea cliffs and sea stacks. Of the latter, Monument Rock on the Lookout Louise Trail is the most spectacular.

As North American climates continued to warm and the continental ice sheets melted further, vegetation changed accordingly. On Isle Royale, spruce gradually took over, first forming scattered open groves and later, dense forests. Following soon came smaller amounts of pine, fir, aspen, and paper birch. With the establishment of these species, the forest must have looked much like the dominant forest on Isle Royale today.

And what of its animals? Many of these, too, probably were species that are present now. In the Great Lakes forests 9,000 years ago roamed marten, fisher, wolverine, lynx, snowshoe hare, beaver, muskrat, porcupine, wolf, woodland caribou, and moose, to name some of the larger ones. But which of these swam, rafted, or crossed the ice to Isle Royale we have no fossil record to tell us. It is tempting to imagine mastodons here, but these great beasts apparently preferred open rather than closed forests, and by 9,000 B.P. they were nearing extinction. One also wonders what they would have thought about crossing ice. The island's complement of insects and birds probably included many of today's. In the shore waters swam trout, herring, and whitefish, cold-water species that had been able to survive near the glacial front.

The warming trend that forced the retreat and eventual disappearance of the continental ice sheets reached a climax some 6,000 years ago. The climate then was warmer and drier than now, and prairie grasslands displaced forests as far east as Ohio, Indiana, and southern Michigan. On Isle Royale this climatic change resulted in the decline of spruce and an increase of pine, oak, maple, and yellow birch. The pollen record in bogs suggests that toward the end of this warm period hemlock, basswood, elm, walnut, and hickory also may have grown on the island, though none of these is present today. Spruce-fir forests probably survived only in cool, wet areas near the shores, in swamps, and on some north-facing slopes, while the deciduous hardwoods covered most of the uplands.

Animal life probably changed in a similar way, with increase of the more southerly species and decrease of northerly ones. Reptiles and amphibians, being cold-blooded and therefore requiring fairly warm climates, quite possibly survived on the island for the first time. Some aquatic species, such as newts and painted turtles, may have been able to swim through the temperate water. Other turtles, frogs, snakes, and salamanders, as well as their eggs, may have been carried on driftwood to these shores. Most probably they came from the Ontario shore to the north and east, since the prevailing currents come from that direction.

Warmer water during this period no doubt also aided fish in crossing the big lake and becoming established in Isle Royale waters. Some larger species, such as pike, may have found a new home throughout the lake, while some smaller ones accompanied rafts of flotsam to sheltered water around the island, and then traveled upstream to interior lakes. At the same time, the cold-water fishes such as whitefish and trout, which probably had become established in Isle Royale

Flora and fauna of Isle Royale, as we know it today, arrived at different times in the island's evolutionary development. The spring peeper may have rafted over on driftwood after the climate warmed; jewel weed was most likely introduced by lake waves or wandering birds.

lakes during colder times, now could not tolerate the warmer inland waters and died off in all but the deepest lakes. Lake trout, for instance, now live only in Siskiwit Lake, while whitefish survive only in Siskiwit and Desor.

About 5,000 B.P., near the end of the warm "pine period," the level of the three upper Great Lakes, now all at the same elevation, stabilized long enough to form another prominent shoreline. This gigantic body of water, known as Lake Nipissing, formed beach ridges, sea arches, and other features on Isle Royale at elevations now from 640 to 660 feet above sea level. (Lake Superior is presently about 600 feet above sea level.) During this stage a bar forming across a cove mouth created Lake Halloran, a sea arch was cut on Amygdaloid Island, and Suzy's Cave, facing Rock Harbor, was carved out by the waves. By this time, with lake levels only 40 to 60 feet higher than now, Isle Royale had nearly reached its present configuration. Siskiwit Lake had been cut off from the big lake by a low ridge, and most of the other inland lakes had also been formed. (In another 3,000 years or so, the present Great Lakes would take shape and Isle Royale

would have emerged to its present extent.)

Isle Royale's biologic story since that time has been shaped by increasing coolness. Spruce-fir forests have spread to all but the highest, driest areas, tightening a noose of competition around the remaining stands of sugar maple, yellow birch, and pine. Whether this trend will continue into another ice age or will shift toward greater warmth, we can only guess. Global warming induced by human-caused "greenhouse gases," a product of increased industrialization and the burning of fossil fuels, may be underway.

Birds and mammals reached Isle Royale by air, water, and ice as plants evolved enough to provide food and shelter. Red crossbills dangle parrot-like on evergreen cones; the red fox may have hunted these parts for as long as 9000 years.

What life inhabits the island at this particular point in its long-short history? Many species for which the climate and habitats are suitable either could not make the trip across or, once arrived, could not become established. Most of the plants and birds of the nearby Canadian mainland have succeeded on the island, but many other forms of life have not. Among the missing vertebrates are black bear, white-tailed deer, raccoon, striped skunk, porcupine, eastern cottontail, and a number of small rodents, as well as snapping turtle, spotted and red-backed salamanders, and leopard frog. The island's wildlife drama today has only a few principal mammal actors: wolf, moose, beaver, red fox, snowshoe hare, red squirrel, and deer mouse; the few other mammals are uncommon or rare. Perhaps the small size of the mammal cast heightens our interest in it; certainly it focuses the action of the play.

Many processes of creation and destruction continue today as they have since rotten ice first melted off this piece of land. Ever so slowly, rock weathers and helps to form soil. Still responding to the removal of its tremendous burden of ice, the northern part of the Superior Basin rises a foot or more per century. Waves carve into the rock shores, make beaches, and build sand bars underwater across coves. Mosses and lichens and the plants that follow create forest on rock. Creeping mats of vegetation form "cataracts" over the "eyes" of lakes and eventually fill them. We witness on youthful Isle Royale the earth's primordial work.

People Come—And Go

*I*f you spend much time at Rock Harbor, chances are you will take a walk out toward Scoville Point on the Stoll Trail. About halfway to the point you will pass three small pits in the rock—a small sample of many pits excavated on Isle Royale by Indians, hundreds of years ago, in their mining of copper. Collectively, they represent man's first appearance on this young island.

In many ways, Indian use of Isle Royale was like most later human activity here: it was seasonal and exploitive, and finally it was abandoned. Unlike other animals, humans have never become permanent residents on this rigorous, remote land.

Indians

As we have seen, plants came soon after the retreat of glacial ice out of the Superior Basin, and animals followed the plants. Close upon the heels of animals came human hunters. By 8000 or 9000 B.P., possibly earlier, Indians had reached the north shore of the lake. We don't know when they first ventured the 15 or 20 miles to Isle Royale; but there is good archeological evidence that, by at least 3500 B.P., they were mining copper on the island. Using rounded beach cobbles, they hammered the rock away from the pinkish veins of pure copper. Perhaps, too, they used fire to heat the rock and make it more friable, though this is uncertain. Probably these early visitors came in small groups during the summer, worked a number of pits, and returned to the mainland for the winter. Quite possibly they burned off the vegetation, as white miners later did, to find the copper veins more easily. They used the malleable metal for spear points and other implements.

For several thousand years, Indians mined copper at Isle Royale, the Keweenaw Peninsula, and other areas around Lake Superior. Some of this material, presumably through trade, found its way to southern Manitoba, the St. Lawrence Valley and New York, and northern Illinois and Indiana; but the chief area of use was eastern Wisconsin. During the period from 2500 to 1500 B.P., the Hopewell Indians of southern Ohio, Indiana, and Illinois used Lake Superior copper to make numerous highly artistic ornaments. We know that Indians used Isle Royale rather extensively during these centuries, since their occupation sites have been found at McCargoe Cove, Chippewa Harbor, Merritt Lane, Washington Island, and other places. Bones uncovered at the McCargoe Cove site indicated some of the contemporaneous animal life: caribou, moose, beaver, lynx, snowshoe hare, muskrat, loon, bald eagle, sturgeon, shorthead redhorse sucker, and turtle.

Judging from the number of sites found, the period from A.D. 800 to 1600 saw the peak of Indian activity on Isle Royale, possibly including copper mining as late as 1500. After the arrival of Europeans in the Great Lakes area, Indian culture began to disintegrate and their numbers declined. During the nineteenth century, small Ojibwa groups remained on the island hunting, fishing, and tapping sugar maples. A few men worked at mines. John Linklater, of Indian and Scotch parentage, and his wife Tcheekeewis, who lived here until they died in the early 1930s, were the last representatives of the Indian race on the island.

In their 4000 to 5000 year use of Isle Royale, Indians apparently left only small pits in the rock as lasting marks on the island. If they burned the plant cover in their search for copper or eliminated beaver or other animals in fur-trade days, there is no evidence of this today. They seem to have left the forests full of wildlife and the waters full of fish.

The same cannot be said quite so confidently for those who followed, though the modern record has been better here than in most places. During the 19th and 20th centuries, people have come for fish, copper, lumber, and finally for that most fragile and elusive of natural resources — wilderness. Even that last quest has left its mark on the land.

Fishermen

In historic times, fishing has been the most enduring economic activity on Isle Royale. The many reefs and miles of shoreline, as well as great range of water depths and several types of bottom material, provide for the varying seasonal needs of lake trout, whitefish, and herring — the chief species sought. Sheltered harbors gave fishermen bases from which to operate.

Commercial fishing began here before 1800, when the Northwest Fur Company took fish from the north side of the island to supply its stations at the western end of Lake Superior. In the late 1830s, the American Fur Company established seven fishing stations on Isle Royale. Their catches were good, but the economic depression of 1837–41 dried

A Fisherman's Life ➤ Milford Johnson, three months old, came to Isle Royale in a clothesbasket on the steamship *America* in 1906. When he was eight or nine he and his brother Arnold began helping their father, a Swedish fisherman. Milford fished Isle Royale until his death in 1980. It was a memorable life. In 1973 I talked with him at his log cabin at Crystal Cove on Amygdaloid Island, but all I remember now is a bear of a man with a gravelly voice and a lot of good stories, a veteran fisherman with a deep respect for the power of Lake Superior. Others recorded his stories and memories in the later 1970s. A few highlights from these books and tapes will sketch his life. ➤ "I tried about all the spots around the island," Milford said, "Rock Harbor, Wright Island, Washington Harbor, Little Todd Harbor." Early on, he fished Rock Harbor for two years with Pete Edisen and for twenty years he fished with his brother Arnold. Milford and his wife Myrtle, who also had been brought to the island as a baby, lived in the Rock Harbor Lighthouse from around 1929 to 1938. For a while he ran a fifty-foot, diesel-powered tug called the *Jeffery.* "In a good day of fishing we'd get a ton, a ton and a half of siskowits" (a fat deep-water lake trout). But it was a long, seventeen-hour day, starting at four in the morning and ending around nine or ten at night, after the fish were cleaned. ➤ In 1956 Milford and Myrtle moved from Star Island, which had been their base since 1938, to Crystal Cove. Then the sea lamprey arrived and nearly wiped out the lake trout and whitefish. "The sea lamprey got so bad that you could lift 10–15 nets and only receive two fish." Many fishermen left the island to fish the Minnesota north shore of Lake Superior, "but we decided to stick it out, fishing herring." By now, their seven children were grown, "so we managed to scrape along. There weren't many of us around the table." But it was hard, tedious work, often lasting until midnight. By the late 1970s, however, the fishing was "as good as ever, about the same per net as when we first came to Crystal Cove, before the lamprey." ▸● Milford's life was not all fishing, as he often recounted with gusto. There were pranks, adventures, and sometimes sheer horror. On December 7, 1927, the *Kamloops* went down near Todd Harbor. Those who made it ashore died of starvation and cold. The following spring John Linklater discovered the bodies and took Milford there. "There was seven of them in a lean-to. One was sitting on a log with his storm clothes . . . just like he was alive. . . . Boy, I'll never get over that." ▸● On another

occasion, Dr. Frank Oastler, making a trip through the interior of the island with Milford, offered him fifty dollars to ride a moose. On Lake Ritchie they paddled up to a bull moose that was swimming across, "and I hopped on. . . . Lying on my stomach, I grabbed him by the antlers." When the moose touched bottom, Milford rolled off quick and swam for the canoe, which "should have been closer. . . . He got his picture—and I got my fifty bucks." ▸● After Milford's death, Myrtle operated the fishery at Crystal Cove until her death in 1987. Two of Milford's sons, Frank and Milford, Jr., helped her and have at times piloted the *Voyageur* or *Wenonah*, boats that bring visitors to the island. The Isle Royale bond continues. ▸●

33

up their markets. After that time, commercial fishing on Isle Royale was continued largely as an individual enterprise, and for the most part it was successful. Nearly every sheltered cove had its fish houses and log cabins, where fishermen and their families lived from spring until fall. Most returned to mainland towns in winter, but a few hardy souls lived here year-round. For biological, economic, and other reasons, including park management policy, fishing declined

Edisen fishery in Rock Harbor circa 1896.

through the present century. In 1972, only four commercial fishermen still operated on the island. And in September 1994, just a few days before he planned to come out for whitefish, lake trout, and herring, eighty-year-old Stanley Sivertson, the last of these fishermen, died. The NPS maintains a small fishing operation at the Edisen Fishery in Rock Harbor to show visitors what it was like.

Lake Superior has not remained the rich source of fish it was when Europeans first settled here. In the 1880s, when fishing was booming on Isle Royale, a decline in whitefish catches was noticed. Whether overfishing was the main problem is not known, but whitefish numbers remained low until recent years, when various management practices helped this resilient species to rebound.

Human activities were directly responsible for a more recent shock to the Lake Superior ecosystem: the building of the Welland Canal allowed sea lampreys to bypass Niagara Falls and enter all the upper Great Lakes. By 1946, these eel-like, parasitic animals had appeared in Lake Superior. They attacked primarily the lake trout and within a few years had decimated its populations, which had already begun a gradual decline from the 1920s through the early 1940s due probably to overfishing. The lamprey also attacked whitefish, driving their numbers down. Fishermen were forced to turn to the herring, a smaller and less profitable species, until they, too, plummeted in the '60s and '70s. Eventually, use of chemical poisons in spawning streams brought the lamprey under control and the lake trout recovered to the point where a small take became permissible. With commercial fishing now under more regulation, whitefish and herring also have recovered.

The introduction of smelt into the Great Lakes about 1912 was deliberate, but this, too, may have had some adverse effects. Smelt proliferated and in spring ran up Lake Superior streams in enormous numbers. Fried smelt make a tasty dish, but, according to many fishermen, they eat large numbers of eggs and fry of other fish, including the larger commercial species. Scientific studies, however, suggested that commercial harvesting levels were more to blame in the case of the herring decline. In any event, smelt populations dropped, for unknown reasons, in the late 1970s and have remained relatively low to the present. Commercial fishing, though virtually ended on Isle Royale, is still a viable occupation in much of Lake Superior, and most of the native fish species around Isle Royale appear to be doing well.

Miners

Of all economic enterprises on Isle Royale, copper mining undoubtedly has had the greatest environmental effects. The chief impact came from the use of fire to remove the plant cover from the rocks. Copper prospectors burned thousands of acres to aid them in their search. In a later chapter we will trace some of the extensive biological effects of such fires. Miners also cut wood for fuel, building material, and mine props, and made clearings for settlements.

The Richard O'Neils in 1892, a mining family at Windigo.

Post-Indian mining occurred only in the nineteenth century, during three periods of activity. The first lasted from 1843 to 1855, after legal cession of land to Euro-American interests in 1842. Much exploration was carried out and over 100 tons of refined copper were obtained, under dangerous and uncomfortable conditions. Two of the more easily seen mines from this period are the Smithwick Mine, a small, fence-rimmed excavation on the Stoll Trail near Rock Harbor Lodge, and the Siskowit Mine, which is on the north shore of Rock Harbor opposite Mott Island.

Interest revived between 1873 and 1881, when larger (but fewer) operations, benefiting from improved mining technology and better transportation, were carried out. The largest of these was the Minong Mine, near McCargoe Cove. Following the lead of the prehistoric miners, who had dug hundreds of small pits in Minong Ridge, workers of the Minong Company sank two shafts and blasted open pits in the ridge. At its peak, production here required 150 men who, with their families, formed a substantial settlement. There was a blacksmith shop, a stamp mill, an ore dock, and railroads between mine, mill, and dock. Today the mine area looks like the scene of some ancient bombing raid. "Poor rock" piles lie huge and bare in the forest. Pits yawn eerily in the side of the ridge. Rusted, twisted tracks go nowhere on their grass-grown roadbeds. Nothing but cellar holes and wells remains of the town. Its site is now occupied by a lovely open forest of aspen, its openness the only obvious hint of the former human presence.

The other substantial operation of this period was the Island Mine, about two miles northwest of the head of Siskiwit Bay. A town was laid out near the mine, and this became the county seat of the newly established Isle Royale County (now a part of Keweenaw County). But fire, low copper prices, and poor deposits cut short the life of the mine. Nothing remains of this town, either. However, the Island Mine Trail, which follows the old road to the mine, passes by the shafts and rock piles, half-screened by the surrounding forest.

The final quest for copper lasted from 1889 to 1893 and centered in the Windigo area. A town was built at the head of Washington Harbor and extensive diamond drilling was conducted to locate the metal, but the deposits proved too poor. The only important product from these efforts was geological data, on which much geological knowledge was subsequently based. Remnants of the Wendigo Mine (1890–92) can be seen on the Huginnin Cove Trail. Thus ended the 4,000-year search for copper on Isle Royale.

Lumbermen

The island's isolation and its shallow soil, which does not allow large stands of tall trees to develop, may have been the chief factors that saved it from intensive lumbering. Aside from the cutting done by miners, there were only two significant episodes of lumbering. In the 1890s a Duluth company cut white cedar and pine along Washington Creek and floated the logs down to Washington Harbor, where they were held in by boom chains. This venture ended when a big storm caused Washington Creek to flood and break the log barrier, sending the harvest out into Lake Superior.

Fire ended the other operation. In the early 1930s, while land acquisition for the newly authorized park was underway, the Consolidated Paper Company was logging spruce and fir from its holdings at the head of Siskiwit Bay. In July 1936 a fire started near the lumber camp and, fueled by slash piles and later joined by two more fires, eventually burned one-fifth of the island. Though 18,000 cords of pulpwood stacked near the bay were saved, much of the company's forest holding was left a charred wasteland.

Tourists and Cottagers

While men sought, rather unsuccessfully, to exploit the island's natural resources commercially, a nonconsumptive form of exploitation—one that would eventually assume dominance—was beginning. Since the 1860s a few tourists had been coming to Isle Royale to enjoy its fishing and its tranquil, remote, romantic wildness. During the early 1900s, with the rapid growth of midwestern cities and the introduction of lake excursion boats, tourism picked up. Resorts were built on Washington Island and at Windigo, Belle Isle, Tobin Harbor, and Rock Harbor. People acquired cottage sites, particularly on the islands and long peninsulas at the northeastern end of the island.

The appreciation of cottagers and tourists for Isle Royale's peace-giving blend of woods and water eventually crystallized into a movement to make the island a park. At first a state park was visualized, but later sentiment favored a national park. In 1922, Representative Louis C. Cramton of Michigan made the proposal in Congress. After a long battle between proponents and opponents, Congress in 1931 passed a bill making Isle Royale a national park project. Lands were gradually acquired and several Civilian Conservation Corps camps were set up to construct trails, fire towers, and the necessary buildings. Isle Royale National Park was formally established in 1940 and was officially dedicated in 1946. Then, as now, occasional foul weather complicated travel to the island. The National Park Service director and assistant director were unable to fly from Houghton for the dedication ceremony; 1,000 others made it by some means.

Isle Royale's preservation as a park was the achievement of many people, but the man who first planted the idea in many minds was Albert Stoll, Jr., a Detroit newspaperman. After a visit to Isle Royale in 1920, he wrote a series of editorials for the *Detroit News* promoting park status for the island. The trail now memorializing him leads past the Indian pits mentioned at the beginning of this chapter to a plaque about Stoll at Scoville Point, thus touching on the first and also the most recent phases in the long human relationship with this island.

Charlie Mott's Last Winter ➤ In the early days of copper prospecting, mining companies hired watchmen to protect their claims during the winter. So it was that Charlie Mott and his Indian wife, Angelique, arrived in July 1843 to watch over a mineral land site in Rock Harbor for the Union Company. They had only been able to obtain "a half barrel of flour, . . . six pounds of butter that smelt badly and was white like lard, and a few beans" before setting out from La Pointe, Wisconsin Territory. Cyrus Mendenhall, the mining entrepreneur and Indian trader who had hired the Motts, promised to send more provisions in a few weeks. They never arrived. ➤ "Having a bark canoe and a net, for a while we lived on fish," Angelique recounted some years later, "but one day about the end of summer a storm came and we lost our canoe; and soon our net was broken and good for nothing also." By Christmas, all the flour, butter, and beans were gone. The ground was frozen hard as stone under the deep snow. They couldn't dig roots any more, just eat bark and a few berries. "Oh God, what I suffered there that winter from that terrible hunger." ►◄ Charlie grew weaker and weaker and then went into a fever. One day he grabbed his butcher knife and began to sharpen it. From the way he looked at her, Angelique thought she "was the sheep he intended to kill and eat." Then the fever passed and Charlie came to himself. But he kept sinking and finally died. Angelique couldn't bury him and she couldn't bear to throw him out in the snow, "but I was afraid that if I continued to keep up the fire he would spoil." So she somehow managed to build another cabin and left Charlie in the first one. Now the worst fear seized her—that she would "take Charlie and make soup of him." She prayed fervently that she wouldn't, and "that the good God would give me something to eat." ►◄ As if in answer to her prayers, snowshoe hare tracks appeared around her cabin, and making snares from her own hair, she began catching the hares. In March she found a canoe cast ashore and mended it. From its sail she made a net and began catching fish. ►◄ In May a boat finally came, with Mendenhall aboard. "He said that he had sent off a batteau with provisions. . . . But the boys told me it was all a lie. I was too glad to get back to my mother to do anything. I thought his own conscience ought to punish him more than I could do." ►◄ Today Mott Island—the park headquarters—and the *Charlie Mott*—a National Park Service landing craft used to haul materials around Isle Royale—memorialize Angelique's unfortunate husband. Her name is on a barge now beached at Windigo. Angelique died at Sault Ste. Marie in 1874. ►◄

What did the people of the United States inherit from the past through establishment of this park? Remarkably much, we can conclude. Humans may have taken most of the beavers and eliminated the lynx and marten from the island by trapping, and probably had diminished the fish populations around its shores. They probably played a role in the loss of the woodland caribou, which disappeared from Isle Royale around 1927. They had introduced some non-native plants, such as clover, and had made clearings in the forest. But generally the activities had not disturbed the normal workings of nature. The fires, though concentrated in time and far-reaching in their effects, perhaps had the same long-term results as the lightning fires that surely have burned this island since it first bore trees. The human occupants had hunted some animals but had not seriously altered the relationships between predators, prey, and vegetation. They did introduce the Norway rat and white-tailed deer, but these did not survive long. In 1946, excluding a few buildings and trails, the island scene and its plant and animal components were probably much the same as they had been four centuries earlier, before Europeans arrived here and set eyes on what they described as "the floating island."

To be sure, however, some natural changes had occurred, particularly among the larger animals. Moose, perhaps present at various times in the past but absent during the nineteenth century, reappeared early in the twentieth. Coyotes were seen and heard through the first half of the twentieth century but disappeared about 1957. And wolves, which probably hunted moose and caribou here in distant centuries, were not regular residents during the 19th and early 20th centuries but became firmly established in the late 1940s. Thus change has continued, with or without the presence of humans, since the island was born.

As commercial fishing disappears and cottage leases expire, old ways of life on Isle Royale fade away. But in some ways the pattern of human activity remains the same. Visitors come for a few days and return home. Park Service people and a few others come in spring and leave in the fall. No one stays permanently. For a week or a season the island attracts us, but in the end the wild forces beneath the beauty send us back across the water. Only for moose and beaver, wolf and raven, spruce and fir is Isle Royale a true home.

The Lake Trout
LAKE SUPERIOR

*M*idway along the south side of Isle Royale, the white, octagonal tower of the Isle Royale Lighthouse rises from its foundation on the rock of Menagerie Island. Under a cloudy October sky, its light flashes warning of the long string of reefs and islands across the mouth of Siskiwit Bay. Half a mile northeast of the lighthouse, at the end of that string of reefs, Glenlyon Shoal lies just beneath the surface, sloping irregularly down to depths of 100 feet and more.

Forty feet down on the shoal, a pair of grey-green, light-spotted lake trout, arched side by side, are spawning, shedding their eggs and milt into crevices and rocky rubble. Not far away, a small sculpin, with large head and bulging eyes, lies propped on its pectoral fins, ready to dart at any smaller prey that happens by. Unfortunately for the sculpin, it has been seen by a burbot, a large, eel-like predatory fish that haunts the bottom of Lake Superior waters. The burbot seizes the sculpin and swallows it, then swims down along the sloping rock to deeper waters. Here and there, tiny, translucent fairy shrimp twitch about over algae-covered rocks, and microscopic plankton drift along in the current that runs by the reef.

Their reproductive task done, the two lake trout leave

their spawn to its fate. Eggs well hidden among the rocks may escape foraging fish and hatch the next spring, but few of the fry will live 6 or 7 years to spawn themselves. The trout move along the reef, watching for smelt, a school of herring, or any other catchable fish. In their hunt they pass two boilers, gangway doors, steel plates, and a long, grotesquely twisted mast, wreckage of the *Glenlyon*, which grounded here in November 1924. To the lake trout, it is only a possible hideout for prey. Overhead, the clouds have parted and the sun sends its rays deep down through the clear Superior water.

*T*hree-fourths of Isle Royale National Park consists of the cold waters of Lake Superior. The lake strongly affects the climate of Isle Royale, its plants and animals, and the lives of its human occupants. Its waters, liquid or frozen, allow or impede the arrival and departure of people and other

Warning of the long string of reefs and islands across the mouth of Siskiwit Bay, the Isle Royale Lighthouse perches on Menagerie Island.

life. The lake makes Isle Royale an island, with all its physical and psychological implications.

What, then, is the nature of this watery environment? First, it is clear, cold, and deep. Low in nutrients, it supports low levels of plankton and other minute life. In summer the currents that run counterclockwise around the island reach only the low 50s (degrees F) at the surface, while 100 feet down the water is at 40 degrees or less. In winter the situation is reversed, with temperatures near 32 degrees at the surface and upper 30s at the bottom. In May–June and again around December, mixing of the water results in roughly equal temperatures from top to bottom.

Many of the parallel ridges of Isle Royale continue underwater for some distance, causing concern for boats of all sizes. But around most of the outer shore the bottom slopes rapidly down to depths of 300 feet and more. The lake trout ranges through most of these depths at one time of year or another, feeding near the surface in spring, moving deeper in summer, and returning to shallower areas in the fall to spawn. It shares the top of the food chain with burbot and introduced species of salmon and trout.

That food chain begins with phytoplankton—blue-green algae, diatoms, and other minute plants. Copepods and other zooplankton, ranging up to fish larvae in size, feed on the phytoplankton. All drift with the currents, unable to propel themselves very effectively, but are most abundant in the upper layers, where light penetrates. In the bottom sediments live various kinds of worms, mollusks, midgefly larvae, and other invertebrates. Tiny freshwater shrimp forage at all levels, moving upwards at night and downward during the day.

Small fish, such as sculpins and smelt, feed on the invertebrates, but so do the schools of bottom-dwelling lake and round whitefish and the sometimes immense schools of vertically flattened lake herring. Similar to lake herring but generally feeding closer to the bottom are several other species of fish collectively known as "chubs." Crowning the food chain, lake trout and burbot prey on all the smaller fish. Young lake trout eat invertebrates, and the bottom-dwelling burbot adds these to its diet at all ages. The introduced rainbow trout now shares the offshore waters and spawns in several Isle Royale streams. Chinook and coho salmon planted near mainland communities of Lake Superior also hunt prey around the island.

Isle Royale fishermen have long distinguished some half dozen types of lake trout. Three types widely recognized by fisheries managers are especially distinctive. The "lean" trout—the most widely distributed form—inhabits inshore areas generally less than 250 feet deep. The "siscowet," more deep-bodied and high in fat content, dwells in basins 150 to over 450 feet deep. And the "humper," intermediate in shape and fat content, inhabits waters around offshore shoals at depths greater than 300 feet. One such deepwater shoal—potential habitat for the humper trout—lies southeast of the east end of Isle Royale. We may be seeing evolution into three separate species, made possible by environmental separation.

Introductions—both deliberate and unintentional—and other human influences have had a huge effect on the ecology of Lake Superior. Isle Royale, because of its offshore location, has been less affected than many other parts of the lake, but only in degree. The introductions of rainbow smelt (intentional) and sea lamprey (unintentional) have had especially big impacts.

The rainbow smelt was first introduced successfully into the upper Great Lakes by a planting in 1912 in Crystal Lake, Michigan. Some of the smelt made their way down a tributary to Lake Michigan and by 1930 the species had appeared in Lake Superior. So rapidly did the smelt proliferate that it became a significant part of the commercial fishery between 1952 and 1980. During this time, lake herring populations collapsed, probably because of two things: overfishing and competition for food with the abundant smelt and the increasing bloater (a deepwater relative of the lake herring). So great was the shift in populations that lake trout turned from herring, their traditional major prey, to smelt. In the late 1970s, for reasons unknown, there was heavy mortality among the older, spawning-aged smelt, and the populations have remained low to the present. During the 1980s, by contrast, lake herring populations rebounded. Fish biologists expect lake trout to turn once again to herring as their main prey.

The sea lamprey is an eel-like parasitic fish. Attacking first lake trout then whitefish, they seriously impacted fishing in Lake Superior from the mid-forties through the sixties when control measures paid off.

The sea lamprey, an eel-like, parasitic fish native to the Atlantic Ocean, made its way into the Great Lakes via canals and perhaps ship bottoms. It was first found in Lake Superior in 1946. The lamprey attaches its mouth—a round sucking disc—to the side of large fish and sucks out their blood and body fluids. Lake trout were the first to suffer. Lamprey populations in Lake Superior exploded during the 1950s and virtually wiped out many stocks of lake trout. "Some places the bottom was white with dead trout," said Milford Johnson, a commercial fisherman on Isle Royale.

Attempts to control lampreys with electrical barriers and traps on their spawning streams were not very effective, but use of a larvicide was—lamprey numbers were cut by 90 percent. Aided by massive stocking of hatchery-reared trout and a several-year moratorium on fishing for it, the lake trout began to come back in the 1960s. On Isle Royale, where no stocking took place, a remnant population of spawners did the job themselves. Today, fishermen say, lake trout are as plentiful as ever around Isle Royale.

Lampreys also attacked lake whitefish, driving their numbers down, but lamprey control efforts, along with harvesting quotas and the whitefish's reproductive resiliency, brought it back, too. "They're as high as they've ever been this century," said Dick Schorfhaar, fishery biologist with the Michigan Department of Natural Resources. The lamprey is probably here to stay, but if the lamprey control measures and regulation of commercial fishing continue to work, the dominant native fishes of Lake Superior should be able to thrive. Stanley Sivertson, who fished commercially at Isle Royale for seven decades, said, shortly before his death, "It's the best fishing I've seen since I was a boy."

Exotic organisms continue to invade the Great Lakes, however. The zebra mussel, for instance, has caused widespread damage in the other Great Lakes, but biologists believe it is not likely to thrive in Lake Superior's cold water. The ruffe, a perch-like fish from Eurasia, was discovered in a tributary river at the west end of the lake in 1987 and since then has been found farther east along the south shore, but the cold, deep, intervening waters are thought likely to prevent its spread to Isle Royale. The ruffe's potential impact on the Lake Superior ecosystem is unknown.

Compared with the other Great Lakes, Superior's water quality is excellent. But not perfect. Industries in the Lake Superior Basin, especially around Duluth and Thunder Bay,

Airborne pollutants fall into Lake Superior— some from regional industries, some from more distant sources. DDT, mercury, and PCBs in levels exceeding Michigan Department of Public Health consumption advisories were found in lake trout sampled at Siskiwit Bay in 1995.

Ontario, cause some water pollution, and air pollutants from distant sources fall into the lake. In fact, experts estimate that some 95 percent of the PCBs (polychlorinated biphenyls) and lead entering Lake Superior are deposited from the atmosphere. Even with its remoteness, Isle Royale is not immune from these effects. Sometimes, with a north wind, you can smell the Thunder Bay pulp mills. Snowfall at Siskiwit Lake was found to have five times the level of PCBs found in similar samples from Duluth and Chicago. And in 1975, many of the Lake Superior lake trout analyzed were found to exceed U.S. Food and Drug Administration limits for human consumption for DDT, mercury, and PCBs. Lake trout from the Isle Royale area appeared to be more contaminated than those in other Michigan waters. However, fish lower down in the food chain—chubs, lake herring, and whitefish—were within the FDA limits. Although contaminant levels in Lake Superior have been trending downward, the Michigan Department of Natural Resources still found causes for concern. Contaminants in lake trout sampled in the Siskiwit Bay area in 1993 exceeded the Michigan Department of Public Health sport fish consumption advisory for total PCBs, total chlordane, mercury, toxaphene, and total DDT.

Acid rain, another widespread concern, has also been detected on Isle Royale. Although acid in the park's rainfall has sometimes been recorded at levels 10 to 40 times higher than normal, calcium-based minerals in the bedrock and soils seem to be adequate to neutralize the effects of acid rain on the lakes and streams.

Although much of the air-borne pollution is probably coming from beyond the Lake Superior Basin, the water-borne pollution of course is not. To maintain and improve the water quality of Lake Superior, Canada and the United States have developed a "Binational Program to Restore and Protect the Lake Superior Basin." More specifically, the goal is to reduce discharge of certain toxic substances to zero through education, demonstration projects, and other methods. Such a goal will require the partnership of state and national governments, industry, municipalities, universities, native groups, environmental organizations, and interested individuals. Isle Royale National Park is participating through its interpretive programs, both on the island and on the Michigan mainland.

While the lake is affected by its surroundings, such as by the pollution that human activity puts into it, the lake, in turn, exercises its own effects. The deep, cold, broad waters of Lake Superior shape the weather and climate above them, which in turn affect air pollution conditions, life around the shores, and human activities on the lake. Most pronounced is the effect on temperature. The cold water cools the air over it in summer and warms it in winter until ice forms, and this climatic effect extends to the surrounding shores.

At its maximum extent, ice cover reaches forty to ninety-five percent of the lake. Usually a large area at the east end of the lake and a strip paralleling the south side of Isle Royale and extending northeastward, remain open. Pack ice comes and goes between the island and the Canadian shore. Occasionally, as in the very cold winter of 1993–94, the entire lake freezes over and a solid bridge to Canada forms, making the journey possible for animals so inclined.

Of most concern to mariners and pilots are the fog, wind, and storms that the lake creates or intensifies. Fog occurs over the lake more than it does inland, but there are great seasonal differences. The most fog comes during June and July, when warm air masses move over the cold lake and moisture condenses. Of the ice-free months, November and December have the least fog. Light winds and fog — most frequent in spring and summer — provide the conditions most conducive to high levels of air pollution. During most of the boating season, daily weather forecasts call for no more than three- to six-foot waves. October and November bring the strongest winds, and on rare occasions these create mountainous waves up to 25 or 30 feet high.

This is the season when the fisherman must weigh high fish prices against the risks of getting the fish, and when many of the Great Lakes shipwrecks have occurred. Six of the ten major shipwrecks at Isle Royale happened between October and December, some on the ships' last voyage of the shipping season. The *Glenlyon*, a 328-foot bulk freighter built in 1893, left Port William on October 30, 1924 with a load of wheat, downbound for Port Colborne on the Welland Canal. Captain William Taylor, in his first season as master of *Glenlyon*, anchored the ship in the lee of the Welcome Islands most of the day October 31

because of a northeast gale, but when it lessened in the afternoon he resumed the voyage. This proved to be unwise, because the wind picked up again, shifted to the north and then southwest, reaching a heavy gale—one of the

worst in years, mariners said. Shortly after clearing Passage Island, the course was altered to run down the south side of Isle Royale toward shelter in Siskiwit Bay.

At about 1:00 A.M. on November 1, the *Glenlyon* struck a reef—now known as Glenlyon Shoal—at the mouth of Siskiwit Bay.

At first the pumps were manned, but when this proved fruitless, Captain Taylor scuttled the ship to hold it to the reef, but for some reason he did not drop the anchors. Two men who lowered themselves in a lifeboat, apparently to inspect the damage, were swept away. Later they were found alive on the shore of Siskiwit Bay. In the afternoon, when the storm had abated, a barge and two sister ships arrived. The crew were all transferred to the *Glenlinnie* and then to the *Glennsannox*. Salvage efforts—except for lightering of some of the wheat—failed. By the next April the *Glenlyon* had bro-

The Underwater experience ➤ Most people come to Isle Royale to walk its trails or boat its waters, but an entirely different experience awaits those who enter the underwater world. Ten major shipwrecks and a number of small boats, includ-

ing local fishing craft of unique design, lie beneath the surface around Isle Royale, preserved by the coldness and easy to see in the clear water. "It's almost a museum of Great Lakes maritime history," said Elenore Maurer, leader of the park's dive team. "There's everything from a wooden side-wheel passenger steamer built in 1871 to more modern steel freighters." Some of the wrecks are nearly intact, but others have been broken and scattered by ice and wave action. ➤ The most pop-

ular shipwrecks for divers are probably the *America* and the *Emperor* because they are so well preserved. The *America* rests on sloping rock in North Gap at Washington Harbor. Her bow is just four feet beneath the surface. As you dive down, the whole steamship gradually takes shape. "It's kind of spooky," said Liz Amberg, the park's Cultural Resource Management Specialist. "You can imagine people walking around, going about their business." The *Emperor*, largest of the wrecked ships at 525 feet, lies on the Canoe Rocks at the northeast end of Isle Royale. Part of its allure is the offshore location and greater depth. The hull broke amidships. The bow section, partly dismembered by ice impact, is encountered at 30 to 80 feet, the intact stern section at 80 to 150 feet. ➤ Besides the intriguing configuration of wrecks, the observant diver will see life. Perhaps a lone lake trout on the hunt, a burbot back in the dark recesses of a wreck, a school of suckers along the bottom, or minuscule hydras and fairy shrimp. Ranger Larry Kangas, down one day, "thought a cloud was passing overhead. I looked up and saw a big school of herring." ▸● What

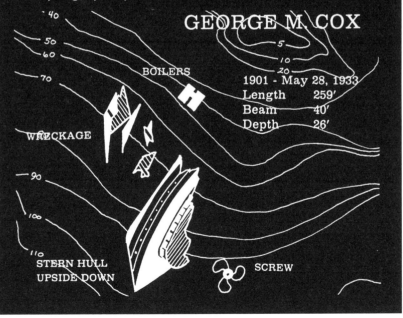

is the appeal of diving? It's not just the excitement of entering a world most people don't see. "I like the feeling of weightlessness," said Maurer. "It's like flying. And I like the heightened awareness—of my surroundings, my partner, my gauges." "It's so peaceful," said Liz Amberg. "You can't hear anything but your own breathing." ▸● Of course underwater explorers must also be aware of safety concerns—weather conditions, the cold water, visibility, and other matters. Park rangers will review these when you get your permit to dive. ▸●

GEORGE M. COX

40
50
60
70

BOILERS

5
10
20

1901 - May 28, 1933
Length   259'
Beam   40'
Depth   26'

WRECKAGE

90

100

110

STERN HULL
UPSIDE DOWN

SCREW

ken in two and completely disappeared below the surface. Today she lies scattered over a distance of 900 feet of bottom, broken up by waves and ice action.

Some other ships that ran aground at Isle Royale were even less fortunate. One crew member drowned when the *Monarch* ran into The Palisades, near Blake Point December 6, 1906. Three officers and nine crew were lost when the *Emperor* struck the Canoe Rocks June 4, 1947. All hands—at least twenty—perished when the *Kamloops* went down near Todd Harbor in 1927, although some made it ashore before freezing and starving to death. And in the worst of all Lake Superior shipwrecks for loss of life, the *Algoma* broke up against the rocks at Mott Island on November 7, 1885; two passengers and twelve crew made it ashore the day after the wreck, but forty-five or forty-seven people were swept away and drowned.

The lake gives life, and it takes away.

The Herring Gull
SHORELINES

*O*n his way down the shore of Rock Harbor, the hiker pauses to admire the scene. Under his feet, lichen-patterned rocks slope down to the lapping water. Down the trail, dark pointed conifers crowd the shore. And beyond the trees, Rock Harbor and its flanking string of islands stretch away to unknown places. Maybe before he leaves the island he will try for trout along this shore, and maybe he will get out to the lake side of those fringing islands to explore the wave-struck rocks. The possibilities of his adventure are endless. But right now he wants to get to Three Mile Camp to make his first dinner. He adjusts the new red pack on his back and continues down the trail.

High in the air above him, a female herring gull surveys the same scene. At the moment, only one aspect of it interests her—the food it might offer. She has two downy young in a nest on Burnt Island, and their demands are incessant. Her keen, cold yellow eyes catch a red spot moving through the trees, but the hiker is not eating anything interesting. She glides down over the docks at Rock Harbor Lodge. The black ducks are there, paddling along the shore, but no one is feeding them. She turns and flies across Rock Harbor toward Raspberry Island.

On the outer side of the island the gull lands on a big rock. All along this shore the gray basalt slopes down from the thick forest to the crashing waves. It is not a very productive place from a gull's point of view, but a surprising amount of life nevertheless exists here. Above reach of the waves and winter ice, lichens, mosses, and crevice plants — three-toothed cinquefoil, harebell, and others — add color to the scene, while closer to the forest edge trailing juniper, ninebark, willows, and other shrubs form a denser cover on the rocks. Under and through the plants, a few ants and spiders search for food, and snails make their slow way. It is mid-June, and a tiny chorus frog, hidden in a mossy pool, is still calling. New tadpoles lie on the silty bottoms of other pools in the rock.

The gull watches disinterestedly as two yellow-rumped warblers fly from the forest down to the water's edge and begin investigating a stranded log. But when another gull drops from the air toward something floating on the water, she takes off screaming and flies at the other bird, driving it away. She settles on the water and begins pecking rapidly at the prize — a dead sucker. Now other gulls arrive to dispute her ownership. Swooping, crying, splashing, they rip at the fish until one retains it long enough to swallow it. The gulls then fly their separate ways, except for the female, who remains on the water to smooth her ruffled feathers.

Nearby a loon hunts where the gull can't go — beneath the water. Here the shore rocks angle down, full of crevices and indentations where lake chubs, sticklebacks, and other small fish hide. The loon passes these and dives deeper, down to the quieter haunts of lake trout, burbot, cisco, and white sucker. It spots a young burbot, and using its wings for extra speed, churns after the fish. Successful, the loon swallows the fish and returns to the surface for air. When the bird tires, it will abandon the pursuit of fish and hunt snails in the shallower water.

Meanwhile the gull has started a patrol flight down the shore. Gliding over Lorelei Lane, the narrow channel that splits the islands into two parallel strings, she sees families of golden-eyes and mergansers swimming near the shores. Each group of downy hatchling ducks is led by its mother, who dives for fish from time to time but never leaves her young for long.

A gull rests on a natural bridge on the rugged shore of Raspberry Island.

Suddenly the gull notices a little red-breasted merganser that has lagged behind. She swoops quickly, but somehow the mother merganser gets there first, and rising almost out of the water, wards off the gull with beak and wings. The gull continues southwestward down the island chain.

At Mott Island she lands on a little gravel beach, one of many that occur on indentations of the shoreline between rocky stretches. High up the beach, near the fringing alders and fir forest, driftwood and other debris lie in tangled rows, cast up by storms. The gull walks deliberately along these rows, now and then turning over sticks and snatching spiders, beetles, and other small things hiding there. Once she tries for a butterfly that has been attracted to the rotting organic mass. But pickings are thin here too. She takes off and wings strongly toward a place that, in the past, has been rewarding.

Even over the old Rock Harbor Lighthouse, the gull knows food is at hand. She has spotted Les Mattson, who operates a demonstration fishery here, walking into the fish house with fish. Just for fun this time, he has been trolling in Middle Islands Passage and has caught three hefty lake trout. The gull is accustomed to Les and lands without hesitation on the end of the dock. Inside the fish

The shorelines of Isle Royale range from tree-lined gravel beaches to bare rocks, as illustrated

in these scenes from Malone Bay, Siskiwit Bay, Mott Island, and the north shore of Isle Royale.

house, Les cleans his trout and drops the entrails into a bucket. When he throws them out, the gull gulps a few pieces down. With a quiet cry she heads toward Burnt Island, near the lighthouse, where her two offspring wait in a shallow nest on the rocks.

Burnt Island, one of many around Isle Royale used by gulls for nesting, is a tall, flat-topped, half-acre rock crowned with a miniature forest of fir, spruce, white cedar, birch, and aspen. It is the home of song sparrows, great blue herons, and many pairs of herring gulls. Most of the gulls build their simple, grass- and moss-lined nests in the open at the edge of the trees. Here, beside a low juniper bush, the female and her mate have hatched and raised two light grey balls of down that now rise on their black legs and with loud peeps greet their mother. Directed by some ancient instinct, they peck at the red spot on her bill until she opens it and regurgitates all she has found this afternoon.

If the food keeps coming day after day, if the weather is not too severe, if they are not killed by a hawk, owl, or another gull, and if they survive three or four winters of southward migration, they may reach adulthood and raise young of their own. But the odds are not good. Perhaps in two or

three years the parents will raise four or five young, and perhaps two of these will live to replace their parents. The environment of which the gulls are a part cannot support all that hatch. Nor can it support all the young ducks or all the insects. The gulls are one of many agents that keep these within bounds. As predator, competitor, scavenger, and prey, the herring gull is an important strand in the Isle Royale web of life.

Her young satisfied for now, the female gull flies northward through other circling gulls, on another search.

*F*or the herring gull, Isle Royale's shore zone means food and shelter — in short, home. For humans, it means beauty, interest, adventure, a place to fish. This meeting place of land and water has a mysterious attraction for us perhaps greater than that of any other island environment. Let's look at it now, as it gradually changes around the island's rim. We will explore the shore not in gull fashion, but as a boater would.

Southwest from Rock Harbor, the basalt humps up steeply from the water, with few gravel beaches for the small boater to land on. Several miles along, a narrow, cliff-walled gap leads into the quiet recesses of Chippewa Harbor.

About two or three miles east of Malone Bay there is a fundamental change in the shoreline, as the surface rock becomes sandstone and conglomerate. Less resistant to the waves than basalt, these rocks make low shores where forest comes down almost to the water. These reddish rocks form the shoreline all the way around to Grace Harbor, at the southwest end of the island.

Malone Bay and Siskiwit Bay, a big scoop out of the island's southern shore, form a distinctive water environment. Islands, reefs, shallows, deep water, relatively sheltered conditions, and collected nutrients make this area attractive to fish, which in turn attract ducks, loons, herons, gulls, cormorants, a few otters, and fishermen. This was one of the chief centers of commercial fishing on Isle Royale, and today it is visited by many sport fishermen in search of lake trout. Some of the islands that string out northeastward from Point Houghton, forming the outer edge of the bay, have been used by gulls for years as nesting grounds. On Menagerie Island, at the end of the string, Isle Royale Lighthouse warns ships of the dangerous reefs.

At the head of Siskiwit Bay lies the longest of Isle Royale's rare sand beaches. Made from fragments and grains of red sandstone and conglomerate, these beaches have a reddish color. Moose often follow these shores, leaving deep cloven hoof prints. Occasionally their tracks are paralleled by those of wolves, which use the beach as a regular pathway because of its convenience. In winter, when ice covers the bay, wolf packs often cut straight across the bay from Point Houghton.

From Siskiwit Bay around to Washington Harbor, there is little shelter for the boater. The prevailing west or south-west wind drives the waves unopposed into the shore. Washington Harbor, with its deep recesses, islands, and nutrient-feeding Washington Creek, forms another "oasis" of shelter and life at the southwest end of the island. Like Siskiwit Bay, it is another gathering spot for fish, fishermen, ducks, moose, and other creatures. Washington Island, at the mouth of the harbor, was long a base for commercial fishermen. At the head of

Storm waves batter an islet near the north end of Isle Royale.

Washington Harbor, Washington Creek brings down organic matter and silt, forming a rich, shallow delta where it enters the harbor. Underwater plants grow thickly on this delta, attracting fish and thus ducks, grebes, loons, and herons. The aquatic plants also attract moose, which come at all times of the day and night to feed on them. Sometimes submerging completely, the big bulls come up with water cascading off their wide backs, chewing contentedly on the succulent "salad." In spring rainbow trout and in fall brook trout run up the stream to spawn.

Washington Creek and Harbor are also good places to watch for otters. These animals have increased amazingly since the years before 1980, when they were seldom seen, and now appear at many places around the shore, as well as inland. The otter renaissance is generally attributed to the rebound of herring—now in abundant supply around Isle Royale's shores.

Stretching from Washington Harbor to Blake Point, Isle Royale's north shore evokes feelings of adventure, respect, and sometimes fear. When strong northerly winds are blowing, the boater has few places of refuge along much of this straight, cliff-lined shore. In the western half, only Huginnin Cove, Little Todd Harbor, and Todd Harbor, each with a campground, offer good shelter. Outside these harbors, the waves can be awesome, beating up against the rock with enough force over the centuries to carve sea caves and arches. Even gulls seem scarcer here, though gulls, herons, and cormorants nest on small offshore islands.

One of the most startling changes boaters and others have noticed in recent years is the explosive increase of double-crested cormorants. This species expanded its range eastward into Lake Superior in the 1920s, but nested in small numbers. Commercial fishermen of the past hardly ever saw one around Isle Royale. Then, beginning in the mid-1980s, more and more appeared each year. Now there are hundreds around Isle Royale's shores. When pressed for an explanation, most people say it's probably because certain toxic chemicals like DDT have been banned and the herring have come back. But why the post-DDT populations are so much larger than the pre-DDT populations is something of a mystery.

One feels like pausing on reaching the security of Mc-Cargoe Cove, a long, straight cleft angling into the island, created by downthrusting of rocks along a fault. At the head of this cove, Chickenbone Creek has formed a delta. The stream winds through dense alders growing on the stream's deposits. This, too, is a rich spot for animals. Here I have watched beavers, a muskrat, ducks, loons, and moose, and once saw a merlin trying to catch blackbirds roosting in the alders.

Continuing on our tour we reach the many-fingered northeastern end of Isle Royale, a seemingly endless alternation of long peninsulas and deep, island-dotted coves. Along these sheltered coves, trees grow nearly to the shore. At the cove heads mussels abound in the quiet shallow water. This is the land-and-water scene that particularly attracted tourists and cottagers in pre-park days. Today Tobin Harbor is the summer home of most of the remaining cottage lease-holders. Gliding past Belle Isle, it is hard to imagine that a (short) nine-hole golf course once lay upon this piece of rock and forest. This is prime ca-

Arctic-alpine plants far removed from their range, including birdseye primrose and the rare black crowberry, are found on rocky shores and islands of the northeast part of Isle Royale.

noe country where the portages are short and the possibilities for exploration are long. Several boaters' campgrounds

Low-Impact Fishing ►⚊ National parks are intended to be kept as natural as possible; that is, as little influenced by humans as possible. That is why, for instance, no hunting is allowed. Fishing, however, has been a traditional use in parks from the beginning, wherever it does not cause significant changes in fish populations. ►⚊ Fishing is certainly a popular activity at Isle Royale and is cited as one reason for establishing the park. At the same time, the park's waters are home to unique, rare, and otherwise valuable fish populations. Several species and subspecies are found nowhere else. For instance, Coaster brook trout—which live in Lake Superior but ascend streams to spawn, are found only here and in a few other locations around Lake Superior. Lake trout have never been stocked at Isle Royale, and several genetically distinct varieties inhabit different environments in the park's Lake Superior waters. All such populations must be protected. Fishing must not be allowed to harm them. ►⚊ Fishing regulations in the park's inland waters are established by the National Park Service, and regulations for Lake Superior are set by the Michigan Department of Natural Resources. The current regulations may be sufficient to protect all the fish populations found here, but more research is needed to make sure. Whatever the regulations, fishermen can voluntarily follow certain practices to sustain the diversity, large size, and large numbers of fish at Isle Royale: *1.* Reduce your daily/possession limit to one fish per day. *2.* Release the larger fish—the important breeding stock. *3.* Keep only one trophy fish per year (it takes about thirty years for a Lake Superior lake trout to grow to thirty pounds). *4.* Quit fishing once you've caught what you're going to keep. *5.* Use one line per person. *6.* Bring fish in slowly from depth; a rapid rise can kill them. *7.* Use single hooks when catch-and-release fishing. *8.* At a minimum, abide by all protective fishing regulations (ask the park for updated information). ►⚊

provide good bases from which to enjoy this watery maze.

At Blake Point, the northeastern tip of the island, rough water often makes trouble for boaters. The water between Blake Point and Passage Island, in fact, is considered some of the worst in Lake Superior. Currents are strong and tricky here, and wind compounds the difficulty. The steep, rocky shore offers no shelter. Once around Blake Point, however, we enter the comparative safety of Merritt Lane, pass the entrance to Tobin Harbor, a long, narrow indentation in the Isle Royale shore, and then return once again to Rock Harbor.

The rocky shores and small islands between Blake Point and Scoville Point are particularly interesting for their arctic-alpine plants, species far removed from their principal range to the north or west in tundra. Some of these are three-toothed cinquefoil, birdseye primrose, yellow mountain saxifrage, and the rare black crowberry and alpine blueberry. Emmet Judziewicz, a botanist from the University of Wisconsin, surveyed all Isle Royale shorelines and found the greatest number of arctic-alpine plants on the south side of the northeast part of the island. "That's perhaps due," he said, "to the sloping nature of the rock, which provides many microhabitats for plants, and to the greater exposure of this part of the shore to cold winds and fog from Lake Superior." The prevailing scientific opinion is that most of these species are relicts of the ice age that invaded from the south shortly after the glaciers retreated, but Emmet thinks perhaps a third of them—especially those with smaller seeds—could have been brought more recently by birds migrating from the Arctic.

Our trip around the island assumes we had a boat big enough to handle the waves, or a kayak. Still, such a trip engenders deep respect for the great lake as well as intimate acquaintance with the herring gull's world.

Fire, Wind, and the Changing Forests

Walking the middle section of the Greenstone Trail, one passes through dense forests of birch and aspen, with few conifers. Here and there, charred stumps twist upward among the white trunks, and fallen pines rot slowly on the forest floor. All these are present signs of the most destructive event on Isle Royale in this century, and of nature's enormous powers of recuperation.

In the summer of 1936, Minnesota, Wisconsin, and Michigan lay in the grip of a deep drought. On Isle Royale, slash from logging operations in the Big Siskiwit River area covered the ground. On July 25, man or lightning started a fire near the logging camp at the head of Siskiwit Bay. The fire eventually burned a large area west of the camp, jumped northward and consumed forests all the way from Lake Desor to Moskey Basin, fueled partly by budworm-killed firs. It was not put out until September, when heavy rains helped the 1,800 firefighters. The fire left 27,000 acres a jumble of charred logs.

But the dense green forest now covering these slopes shows that nature can cope with fire. Fire, in fact, is a part of nature, an element to which plant and animal species have become adapted. Other forces, too, attack the forests, and

form a part of the total pattern of life. Paper birch and aspen are often pioneer trees, Wind blows trees down; insects devour creating a new forest on leaves and tunnel through trunks; disease Isle Royale in burned enters; animals browse saplings or cut areas. trees. All these agents keep the forests in slow turmoil, in continual cycles and subcycles of destruction and re-creation.

Indeed, more than half of the forest on Isle Royale is in some stage of recovery from fire and other destructive forces — not yet having reached a mature stage in which certain tree species have attained long-term dominance. The process of succession toward that state is continuous; but disturbances, particularly the strong winds, work against the attainment of a mature, stable forest over the whole island. Instead, there is a patchwork of forest types, generally following the linear pattern of ridges and valleys but made more random by the chance effects of destructive forces.

On most of Isle Royale — that part most affected in the

growing season by the layer of cool, moist air over Lake Superior—the trend is toward a forest of white spruce and balsam fir. Sizable patches approaching this type, though containing much birch and aspen, occur near the shorelines. Forests of old aspen and paper birch in which spruce and fir have not yet become dominant occupy a larger area. On the central ridges in the southwestern part of the island, where soils are fairly deep and the climate is somewhat warmer, mature forests of sugar maple and yellow birch have stood for a long time, apparently little affected by fire. This type and spruce-fir represent the two main types toward which the forests trend. Most of the 1936 burn area will probably progress toward these two kinds of forest. Other types on the island are swamp forests of black spruce, white cedar, and fir, and small areas of jack pine on some rocky, south-facing slopes and ridgetops. These forests may eventually join the dominant white spruce-fir forest, as swamp soils dry and spruce grows up in the shade of the pines.

When fire strikes hard, burning trees as well as ground cover, it sets back succession to an early stage. Where fire is particularly intense, it may consume all organic matter in the soil and, together with the erosion that often follows, strip the surface down to bare rock. But in most places some ash-covered soil is left. From this, grasses, fireweed, pearly everlasting, and other herbaceous plants soon sprout, speckling the blackened earth with green. These are followed by woody plants: thickets of hazelnut, seedlings of juneberry, fire cherry, and chokecherry. Paper birches, aspens, and mountain-ashes, killed above ground, resprout from stem and roots below ground, sending up several shoots in place of each single stem burned. In a few years an open grassy area, dotted with shrubs and small trees, has developed.

Grasshoppers, flies, bees, chipping sparrows and song sparrows find such places to their liking.

As shrub clumps and tree sprouts grow over the fire-felled logs, making a dense tangle of greenery, snowshoe hares take advantage of the combination of food and cover, and red foxes take advantage of the hares. Moose find a lot of browse in such places, and wolves find moose.

If conditions are right, the trees grow rapidly. Gradually the shrubs are shaded out, the logs rot, and lower tree branches die, reducing the amount of food that hares can reach and eliminating many of their hiding places. After thirty years or so, the trees may be too tall to supply food even for moose. At this stage, the forest is a monotonous, even-aged stand of close-packed young birches and aspens, with a few small spruces and an occasional fir underneath, the result of seeds blown or carried in from older forests. Here and there a white pine shoots up, perhaps one day to tower above all the other trees. The forest floor, now fairly well shaded, is likely to be covered with thimbleberry, large-leaved aster, bracken fern, and wild sarsaparilla, with perhaps a few bunchberries and bluebead-lilies underneath them. As might be expected from the lack of variety in habitats, animal life is rather scarce. One may see only an occasional red squirrel or moose, and a few birds such as red-eyed vireos, ovenbirds, and chickadees. But diversity will grow with age.

This stage may be slow in developing, however, because of heavy browsing by moose, which can prevent big patches of aspen and birch from growing more than a few feet tall. Through all stages of growth, in fact, moose strongly affect the structure and composition of the forest.

On some burned areas, particularly dry slopes and ridgetops, spruce and jack pine, rather than birch and aspen, are the pioneer trees. In such places there may be little change in the tree species present as the stand grows older.

In a typical stand of young birches and aspens, competition among the trees for water, light, and minerals gradually thins the stand as the survivors grow taller. Spruces and firs, now germinating more abundantly, begin to create a dark layer beneath the birches and aspens. The firs, however, may be under continual pressure from moose browsing, and few will "escape" to become part of the overstory. (However, where moose are few, as on Smithwick and Raspberry Islands, many firs will escape and predominate over spruce.)

A. MORRIS / VIREO

Mature forests provide homes for a variety of bird species like the winter wren, magnolia warbler, black-capped chickadee, and common yellowthroat.

A hundred years or more after the fire, the spruces, along with some firs, may gain dominance over the deciduous trees. Gradually the aspens reach the end of their life span. Where the conifers stand close together the aspens have few offspring, for here the forest floor is too shady for survival of the seedlings or root suckers. Paper birches, usually more numerous, survive longer as a forest component, but their seedlings and root sprouts have the same problem. Given enough time and lack of disturbance, most of the birch would disappear, too, and a dark forest consisting entirely of spruce and fir would develop. For a number of reasons (stated earlier and which we will examine later) this seldom happens on Isle Royale.

These maturing forests, with their mixture of conifers and broad-leaved trees, provide homes for much more wild-life than do the dense young stands. Red squirrels, attracted by the seeds and thick cover of conifers, become common. Warblers, thrushes, red-breasted nuthatches, winter wrens, white-throated sparrows, and many other birds occupy the variety of niches now available.

If the area is above the influence of the layer of cool moist air that lies over Lake Superior, it may change from a

young paper birch-aspen stand into a sugar maple-yellow birch forest rather than spruce-fir. In this case, a dense crop of sugar maple seedlings develops under the birches and as-pens, and the maples, with a sprinkling of yellow birches, eventually take over. In some areas, red maples, red oaks, and white pines may be important in the successional stages; and white pine may last for many years in the mature stage. In the mature maple-birch forest, which shelters a few coni-fers in moist places, squirrels and birds are also much more abundant than in the earlier stage of the forest, though this type seems to have less variety of wildlife than does spruce-fir forest.

The relative variety and abundance of life in the later stages of forest succession is due partly to the several layers within them. There is the canopy, high above the ground and struck with sunlight. There is an understory, composed mostly of young of the canopy trees. There are shade-loving shrubs and small plants near ground level. But the variety is due also to destructive forces, which create openings in the forest and thus provide additional habitats.

Besides fire—which burns small areas much more often than large ones—wind, insects, larger animals, and disease contribute to the constant change in forest structure. Wind, aided by thinness of soils and trunk-weakening diseases, probably takes the lives of more trees than does any other agent. Over most of Isle Royale, the last glacier was stingy with its deposits, and there has not been enough time since then for deep soils to develop. The shallow root systems of spruce and fir, anchored in thin, often wet soil over rocks, provide poor resistance to strong winds. Particularly during fall storms or high winds in winter, when trees may be laden with ice or snow, trees fall by the hundreds. Balsam fir is frequently afflicted with heart rot and this adds to its susceptibility, often causing it to snap off in high wind. Blowdowns are thus a common sight on Isle Royale, creating barriers for the hiker, cover and food for animals, and many openings in the forest.

Insect outbreaks periodically add their effects to those of other agents of destruction, such as disease. In the early part of the twentieth century many tamaracks were weakened by larch sawfly larvae, which eat the needles, and tamaracks are still scarce on the island. In the 1930s the spruce budworm attacked many firs (which it prefers over spruce) in the same manner, and it periodically returns. In 1994 the budworm defoliated some 6,800 acres of fir and spruce. The chief insect scourge of the early 1970s was the large aspen tortrix (a close relative of the spruce budworm), which eats the leaves of aspen before making its cocoon inside a rolled-up leaf. Many acres of aspens, particularly on the southwest end of the island, were defoliated; but most of the trees leafed out again. On a small scale every year, and on a large scale some years, insects contribute to the constant forest turnover.

Less dramatic but perhaps more important in the total effect on trees are diseases. Heart rot, mentioned earlier, is caused by fungi that enter the heartwood of trees. White pine blister rust, another fungus, kills white pines by destroying needles and girdling stems. Hundreds of other fungi, bacteria, and viruses attack trees, continually challenging their fitness to live and to dominate the area they shade.

The role played by vertebrates in forest change is especially evident on Isle Royale. Moose and beaver drastically affect the structure and composition of the forest, while other mammals, though by comparison unimportant agents, nevertheless have measurable effects.

In winter, moose feed extensively on the foliage and twigs of fir. The island's high population of moose has left browse lines on most stands of fir, denuding many of the branches from the snowline to about eight feet above the ground. This heavy browsing of fir has the net result of decreasing the fir component of the forest and increasing the proportion of spruce, which moose do not eat, perhaps because of the sharp-needled leaves. At the southwest end of the island, moose are virtually removing fir as a forest component. The canopy firs are dying through normal aging, and moose browsing is preventing young firs from reaching cone-bearing size. You can see this dramatically at a fenced exclosure near the Windigo ranger station. Inside the exclosure, a dense mixture of firs, birches, and other trees reaches skyward. Outside it, there is little but the gray, chewed-up stems of stunted saplings.

Moose are also especially fond of aspen, mountain ash, paper birch, fire cherry, mountain maple, and red maple; in some areas they keep saplings of these species perennially browsed back to shrub height. Earlier in this century, moose almost wiped out the American yew, an evergreen shrub that once formed dense thickets on the island. Only on certain offshore islands, such as Raspberry and Passage, where moose seldom or never go, does yew continue to flourish. Elsewhere, since moose eat the more conspicuous individuals, only small specimens of yew can be found. In a later chapter we will further examine the moose-vegetation relationship on Isle Royale.

Moose and beaver drastically affect the structure and composition of Isle Royale's forests.

Beavers, of course, dramatically change the forest in the vicinity of their ponds, which in some areas of Isle Royale, such as the northeast end, form a large part of the landscape. Trees are killed in the flooded area, and many aspens and birches within 150 feet or more of the pond are felled. The beavers thus maintain open areas in the forest, and to some extent encourage the growth of spruce and fir through the removal of aspen and birch. Intense suckering—sprouting of shoots from the base of a trunk—occurs when beavers cut aspens.

Snowshoe hares feed on many of the same plants that moose eat, but their comparative effect on vegetation is small. As with moose, they have the greatest impact on the forest in winter, when only woody stems, twigs, and bark are available to the hares. Since they can reach about two feet above the surface of the snow, they browse up to a height of four or five feet.

Insects, birds, and mammals also play a productive role in the forest. Insects aid in seed production by pollinating flowers. Birds and mammals disperse seeds and aid in germination by burying some and softening the coats of others in their digestive tracts.

The forest, then, is an ever-changing mixture of plants, acted upon and influenced by all the forces of the environment, including the whole spectrum of animal life that dwells within it. While hiking on Isle Royale, particularly on trails that cut across the topographic grain, one sees a mosaic of forest types and stages: damp shoreline forests of fir, spruce, and birch dripping with beard moss; open, shrub-dotted stands of tall aspens and birches; dense, dark swamps of black spruce and white cedar; sun-baked grassy ridgetops, slowly recovering from some long-ago fire. Each part of the forest is coming from somewhere and going somewhere. None of it is standing still.

One purpose of national parks is to preserve places where nature is allowed to operate as much as possible without human interference. On Isle Royale, this *laissez-faire* policy extends even to fire. Though human-caused fires are put out, lightning fires are monitored very carefully but allowed to burn unless they threaten some campground or other developed area. Most of these are very small and go out soon.

Similarly, insect outbreaks are not checked. Nature

eventually does this herself, through the effects of weather, food shortage, and predation by other insects and birds. For instance, the population explosion of the large aspen tortrix in the early 1970s was inhibited, if not checked, by an army of birds, including red crossbills, blackbirds, many kinds of warblers, and even woodpeckers that awkwardly crept out on the twigs and picked caterpillars off the leaves.

On Isle Royale, as in all wild places, the forces of creation and destruction work in some ultimate balance. This equal struggle of life against death creates many different patterns of existence in the woods and waters of this lonely, harsh, beautiful island.

The Red Squirrel
SPRUCE-FIR FOREST

Bird song and the gray light of dawn wake the red squirrel, curled in his grass-lined, leafy nest in an old woodpecker hole. He climbs out, sits on a branch of the dead birch that is his current home, and surveys his domain.

The acre he claims lies on top of a low ridge along the Stoll Trail, half a mile east of Rock Harbor Lodge. An open, parklike forest of spruce, fir, birch, and a few aspens covers the ridge. Underneath, sapling firs outnumber the young spruces, but many of the firs have been heavily browsed by moose, leaving the upper stems bare of branches. Large-leaved aster, thimbleberry—with its big, maplelike leaves— wild sarsaparilla, Canada dogwood, scattered blue-bead lilies, and clumps of low juniper bushes cover most of the ground, but not thickly. Moss grows on rotting logs and stumps. On the north side of the ridge, where the underlying rock tilts steeply down to the shore of Tobin Harbor, moss, other ground plants, and young conifers are thicker, encouraged by the greater moisture. Here old stumps of aspen, cut by beavers years ago, are beginning to rot. On the south side, where the rock slopes gently but faces the sun, the ground cover is scarcer, and includes some reindeer lichens on the rock and patches of bracken fern. At the foot of the slope lies a swamp, draining slowly between this little rise and the next. Here tall black spruces cast shade on the grasses, ferns, horsetails, and broad-leaved skunk cabbage that cover the wet ground.

The red squirrel, which feeds on the seeds of conifers, is found in coniferous forests across North America from Nova Scotia to Alaska.

It is the third week in June. All the summer birds are back and are insistently proclaiming their territories. To the squirrel's ears come the ringing song of an ovenbird, the sweet loud whistle of a white-throated sparrow, the flute-like rising swirl of a Swainson's thrush. Nashville, magnolia, yellow-rumped, blackburnian, and black-throated green warblers add their small but distinctive songs to the early-morning chorus. Down in the swamp, a winter wren unwinds its tinkling medley, and a little yellow-bellied flycatcher quietly whistles, "pur-wee." Intermittently, spring peepers peep.

None of these sounds is important to the squirrel, though they indicate the general locations of nests he might rob. But then a long, chattering "tcher-r-r-r" from down in the swamp electrifies his nerves. "Tcher-r-r-r!" he answers, vibrating with excitement and twitching his tail. It is another squirrel, one of two that occasionally wander up the slope into his territory. He calls again, angrily. Hearing no answer, he starts down the tree to begin the morning's foraging.

Many plants in the forest have something to offer him at one time or another, but now in early summer he is concentrating on the tender buds at the tip of spruce twigs. Stopping briefly on a log to nibble a bracket fungus, he then leaps up onto the trunk of a large spruce and scampers to its top, hardly pausing. For a half hour he carefully examines each branch, crawling out each one until it threatens to drop him. Then, surfeited with buds, he races down the trunk and out a limb, and winds through a succession of tree tops until he is above the top of the north slope. A crunching sound has roused his curiosity, and investigate he must. Below, half hidden in the foliage, a cow moose is stripping the leaves from young birches and noisily chewing them. Behind her, two small, light-brown calves nibble tentatively at ground plants. With the moose population high, most cows have borne only one calf, but these two seem to be thriving. For a week now the calves have followed their mother up and down Scoville Peninsula, sometimes swimming across short stretches of water but seldom leaving the peninsula. Chances are that they will escape wolves this summer, because the pack on the island's northeast end seldom comes near the lodge area during the busy season. Two young bulls, and occasionally a yearling cow, wander through the squirrel's territory from time to time. He chatters at the trio below him, but they pay no attention.

Getting no response here, he works his way through trees and along the ground to a little grove where an aspen stands. Climbing the trunk he reaches a hole just as a downy woodpecker pops into it to feed four noisy young. The squirrel scurries around the hole excitedly, then loses interest and descends to investigate the ground.

Restlessly he bounds along the forest floor, through plants, along logs, then pauses, investigates under an old stump, emerges and continues. He knows every foot of his acre—what food it offers, what hiding places for himself and his seed stores, what possible nesting places. He also knows its dangers. A few woodpecker feathers lie scattered near the trail where some hawk or owl has feasted; it could have been squirrel fur. An old thigh bone of a hare under a juniper bush wakes an image of a red fox kill he witnessed here the past winter. The fox is a frequent visitor, forcing the squirrel to be ready always to dash for a tree or tunnel. Mink and weasel are occasional threats, but the marten, scourge of red squirrels through much of the north woods, is rarely seen on the island. The deer mouse whose territory overlaps the squirrel's is a night animal, subject to attack by weasel, mink, fox, and especially owl. With alertness and luck, the squirrel may live two or three years. The mouse will do well to see another spring.

The squirrel pauses on a log to rest. Near him a bumblebee sprawls on the white bloom of a bunchberry. The late morning sun sparkles on the transparent wings of a hovering dragonfly, before it dives at a mosquito dancing in the air. There is an endless supply of mosquitoes; but there are also many birds that catch dragonflies. The dragonfly's chances for lasting the season are much less than those of squirrel or even mouse.

Feeling a certain lassitude in the warm sun, the squirrel climbs up a favorite spruce tree and stretches out on a limb where he can soak up the sun's rays. On the trail beneath him a little red-bellied snake also lies stretched, taking in the sun. Like regular second hands of some giant clock, herring gulls fly over on their patrols of Tobin and Rock Harbors, drawing shadows through the dappled forest. Less often, ravens in ones and twos skim the tree tops, croaking as they pass. So familiar are these birds, the squirrel pays no attention. Suddenly a shape comes gliding *under* the tree tops. The squirrel tenses for flight, but the broad-winged hawk sails past him and lands on a branch over a small grassy pool. For several minutes it sits hunched and still. Then it drops toward a green frog at the edge of the pool. But at the last moment the frog dives; it will not today feed hatchling hawks a mile away on Minong Island.

Especially adapted to flight *through* forests, rather than over them, the broad-winged hawk is a top predator of this ecosystem.

Some time later, after the hawk has left, the squirrel resumes his rounds. It is an uneventful afternoon, except for a short chase when he surprises one of the squirrels from the swamp raiding a food cache. The sun drops toward the ridge behind Tobin Harbor. Sitting beside the Stoll Trail, the squirrel feels vibrations. A human family comes by. He runs up a small tree and chatters at them. They stop to look, then walk on. As the sun touches the top of the ridge beyond Tobin Harbor, the squirrel starts toward his nest in the dead birch. He has successfully completed another day.

*T*his particular squirrel's patch of forest, though unique like every other patch, has many elements found throughout Isle Royale's spruce-fir stands. The variations in these stands consist mostly in the proportions of the plants and animals common to all of them. The abundance of the constituent plants and animals in turn is determined by the moisture, soil, and sunlight, and by the history of the immediate area—recentness of fire, wind damage, intensity of moose browsing, and other things. All of these factors are strongly influenced by the stand's topography and its location with respect to the Lake Superior shoreline.

Forests near the shore are the moistest and also most subject to wind damage and moose browsing. The cold waters of Lake Superior cool the adjacent layer of air and contribute moisture to it. This cool, moisture-laden air inhibits evaporation in the shoreline forests, thus allowing most of the moisture in the soil to remain there to be used by plants. A plus factor for tree growth, this is counterbalanced

Shoreline forests are kept damp and cool by the lake influence, but are vulnerable to wind damage and moose browsing.

by the effect of wind, which can sweep across the wide expanses of the lake and hit the shore full force, toppling many trees. Shoreline forests also receive the heaviest winter browsing by moose, because these animals find here the greatest quantity of fir, a favorite winter food, and, because of the roof effect of close-packed conifers, somewhat lessened snow depths.

The result near shorelines is a damp forest of small trees with a high proportion of birch, which often springs up in wind-created openings; a high proportion of fir, which would be more numerous without moose; scattered white spruce trees that are usually, because of greater resistance to wind-throw, taller than the firs; a sprinkling of mountain-ash and white cedar; and a generally thick, diverse cover of ground plants and shrubs. Old man's beard, a lichen resembling Spanish moss and dependent on high moisture, festoons the trees. Mott and Raspberry Islands have especially good examples of shoreline forest.

Inland and higher up, as the lake influence diminishes, temperatures become higher, thus increasing evaporation. Wind is reduced by the buffering effect of ridges and by the intervening expanse of the forest itself. Old man's beard disappears. In sheltered valleys, trees can grow fairly tall.

One of the most noticeable changes inland is the increase of spruce and decrease of fir. Bob Janke, retired professor of biological science at Michigan Technological University, believes this is due to differences at the surface of the soil. "Near the shore," he says, "decomposition of organic matter is slow on the cool ground. The litter of twigs, needles, and dead plants may become several inches thick. This layer of litter, filled with air spaces, tends to dry out fast after a rain, making a poor bed for tree seeds to germinate and grow on. But fir seeds are larger than those of spruce, providing more food for the seedlings and more time for the roots to reach mineral soil and its moisture." Fir is also more tolerant of shade. So, in the shore zone, more fir seedlings survive to become trees.

Inland, warmer temperatures speed up decomposition, reducing the depth of the litter layer. The drier soil supports fewer trees, which shed less material onto the forest floor. The relative dryness makes for more frequent and intense fire, which often produces open areas with mineral-rich soil. Spruce is better able than fir to germinate and grow under these conditions and thus is more abundant inland.

The spruce-fir situation illustrates one aspect of the intense competition between plants on the forest floor. In many places, the growth is so thick that tree seedlings of all species can get started only on rotten logs, stumps, or mossy rocks.

The ground cover in spruce-fir forests varies greatly, depending mainly on the amount of moisture and sunlight present. Where conifers stand close together, shutting out the sun, the forest floor is nearly bare of plants. Where the

canopy is more open, the ground is likely to be covered with mosses, club-mosses, ferns, and a wide variety of herbaceous plants, such as Canada dogwood, wild sarsaparilla, big-leaf aster, star-flower, twinflower, wild lily-of-the-valley, bluebead lily, and fringed polygala. Orchids, though less common, are frequently found; calypso orchid and spotted coral-root are among those forest species seen most often. In northern coniferous forests such as those on Isle Royale, many of the ground plants are evergreen—an adaptation to the short growing season. The wildflowers bloom abundantly through July, unlike those in the deciduous forests far-

Wild lily-of-the-valley and coral root (opposite) are two species of herbaceous plants that grow on the floor of open conifer forests of Isle Royale.

ther south, where the majority of flowers blossom in spring before unfurling tree leaves shut out most of the sunlight.

The common shrubs include squashberry, red-berried elder, and bush honeysuckle. Where the forest is particularly open or contains much birch and aspen, thimbleberry abounds. This big-leaved plant with the red, raspberry-like fruits has an odd distribution. It occurs around the northern Great Lakes and from the Rocky Mountains northward and westward. Devilsclub, a spiny shrub restricted on Isle Royale to Blake Point, a few islands at Rock Harbor, and Passage Island, has an even more disjunct distribution. It occurs in a few places around Lake Superior, but its principal range is in the Pacific Northwest. The favored explanation for the split distribution of these two species is that in early post-glacial times, when a cool, wet climate stretched all the way across the continent, they had a continuous distribution; when a warmer, drier climate expanded the central grasslands, the area where these plants could grow was cut in two. Climatic change is often a suspected factor when a plant or animal has such an odd range.

A walk through these forests of spruce, fir, aspen, and birch is enlivened by encounters with animals. We meet the red squirrel most often; in fact, it seems to be everywhere. Squirrel populations on Isle Royale are higher than on the mainland, although one litter a year, averaging three young, is the rule (compared with two litters averaging more young in other areas). The lack of an efficient predator on squirrels, such as the marten, may be an important reason why Isle Royale's populations are so high. Red squirrels prefer mature forests where conifers abound, though their numbers are also high in sugar maple forests. Conifer seeds and fungi are their staple foods, but they also eat many other things, including seeds, flowers, fruits, and roots of various plants, as well as insects and carrion. Amazingly, fewer young are born in poor cone years, though development of the cones occurs after the breeding season. Apparently, the females can detect early signs of cone production and in poor years avoid or inhibit conception.

Early or late in the day you may surprise a snowshoe hare nibbling some trailside plant. These animals occur where there is thick cover, such as low-spreading conifer boughs, windfalls, or dense shrubs. The population fluctuations of snowshoe hares are famous, though not well understood.

Farther north, in Canada, the cyclic swings are enormous; on Isle Royale these are damped but still quite noticeable. The cycles usually last about 10 years, although Isle Royale's are much less regular.

Snowshoe hares seek thick cover such as low-spreading conifer boughs, but will venture out in the spring to nibble young plants.

Peaks on the island occurred in 1953, 1963, but then not again until 1988.

The deer mouse is the only small rodent on Isle Royale. Of the half dozen or so species of small rodents occurring on the nearby Canadian mainland, this is the only one that has bridged the water gap. Why this and no others is a mystery. Deer mice live throughout the island now but seem to be most abundant in coniferous forests. Individual deer mice, like squirrels, maintain territories that range from about one-half to one acre in size. The resulting density of deer mice is thus quite low in comparison with that of some other small rodents that occur elsewhere and may explain the scarcity of owls on Isle Royale.

The red fox preys on squirrel, hare, and mouse, but hares are usually its mainstay. Squirrels and mice are relatively unimportant fox food here, since the energy gained from them seldom justifies the energy required to catch them. Occasionally muskrats are caught, but these, too, figure in the diet in a small way, as do frogs, snakes, fish, and insects. Isle Royale's foxes turn their main attention from hares only in late summer, when they gorge on fruits, particularly the dark blue berries of wild sarsaparilla. In winter, they supplement their diet with moose meat scavenged at wolf kills. Your chances of seeing foxes are good, since many of them have become accustomed to people at developed areas, and some, unfortunately, have become panhandlers and camp robbers.

Like fox, hare, squirrel, and mouse, moose are found over virtually all of Isle Royale. Being dependent on moose, wolves, too, course the whole island. You are quite likely to meet moose, especially around lakes and ponds; but wolves are the island's needle in a haystack. With luck you may hear them howling, and with greater luck catch a glimpse, but for most people they are simply an unseen presence in the forest, adding to it a special dimension of wildness.

A Fir Tree's Life ➤● In late October along the shore of Rock Harbor, a gentle northwest wind carries the winged seeds of fir down to the forest floor. A month later, smaller spruce seeds are drifting down. In one spot a fir seed germinates and sends its roots down through leaves and twigs to the dark humus below. A foot away two spruce seeds have fallen. One germinates but dies before its roots can reach through the litter to the moist soil below. The other spruce seed is eaten by a deer mouse, which prefers spruce seed over fir. ➤● During the first few years the fir's tap root grows down a short distance and then sends reddish lateral roots out through the humus. On the shady floor, the stem grows up a foot or two, putting out whorls of branches with flat foliage. Sheltered by others of its kind, and half buried by snow, at first it escapes the winter browsing of moose. But when the outer firs have been stripped half bare and the young fir is three feet high, a moose finds it. Over many summers the fir grows, only to be nipped back in winter by moose. After 30 years, the fir is only four feet high. ➤● But then the moose population

declines and the fir is left alone. It shoots up, extending above its fellows up toward the open forest canopy of spruce and birch. At age 50, the fir is 30 feet tall. Beard moss hangs from its dead lower branches. The live branches are now well out of reach of the occasional moose that passes by. Warblers and kinglets feed in its branches but nest in nearby spruces, which have denser foliage. The fir has been shedding seeds for 10 years, and some have sprouted and lived. ➤● At age 70 it is 50 feet tall,

almost even with the old paper birches and spruces in this forest. But now a tiny enemy appears. Spruce budworm populations have been building up and each year defoliate more of the fir trees. By the time the budworm peak has passed, the damage has been done. Weakened, the fir suffers fungus attack. Heart rot spreads through the now old fir, and one day in November a northeaster breaks it in half. ➤● For some years the half-trunk stands, furnishing a home for a pair of hairy woodpeckers. The rest of it lies rotting on the ground, returning its nutrients to thimbleberries, blue-bead lilies, and a few small fir trees. ➤●

The Black-Throated Blue Warbler
MAPLE-BIRCH FOREST

Nervously the warbler works its way toward the tip of the branch, now peering under a leaf for insects, now cocking its head to look skyward for hawks. In a world of green and gray and brown, it is easy to spot. Pale blue-gray mantles its head and back; a band of black runs from its face to its flank; its breast and belly and the spot at the bend of each wing are pure white. To a hawk, it would be a small but conspicuous morsel.

The green, shady world of this particular black-throated blue warbler is a small piece of the forests of sugar maple and yellow birch that blanket Isle Royale's southwestern highlands. The warbler lives at one end of a rise in the undulating crest of Greenstone Ridge, about three miles from Windigo. The trees atop this steep-sided, elongate, five-acre knoll are mostly sugar maples, with some yellow birches and miniature groves of white cedar, while on the relatively level, partly wet ground at its base there are more yellow birches and some firs among the maples. It is a highly structured world: dense canopy above; next an open layer with lots of flying room; below that a layer of foliage ten to twenty feet above the ground formed by a multitude of sugar maple saplings; another open, nearly shrubless layer beneath that; and on the leaf-covered ground few plants but the tiny seedlings of sugar maple.

The warbler shares this shady knoll with two more mated black-throated blue warblers and with several other species of birds. There are pairs of blue jays, Swainson's thrushes, hairy and downy woodpeckers, black-capped chickadees, black and white warblers, and broad-winged hawks. The red-eyed vireo, black-throated green warbler, and ovenbird are each represented by three pairs. Living amongst the birds are three red squirrels. Each species uses the hill's resources in a different way, gleaning different kinds of food from it or searching only certain parts of it. The squirrels, for instance, hunt mostly seeds and buds, the thrushes and ovenbirds work the ground for insects, the woodpeckers drill tree trunks for the larvae within, the red-eyed vireos search the sapling foliage and the canopy for insects, and the broad-winged hawks hunt everywhere—for squirrels, birds, and, especially in the wet places around the knoll, for frogs and snakes.

The creatures of each species, except the hawks, claim only a part of the knoll, a piece big enough to provide food for themselves and their young. This territory they defend against others of their kind, which otherwise would compete with them for food. For the hawks, however, the knoll is only a small part of their territory, which extends over two or three square miles.

The black-throated blue warbler rarely sees vertebrate animals other than these. Occasionally a moose wanders through, browsing on young sugar maples as it goes. Hares that headquarter in the swampy woods nearby sometimes venture to the foot of the slope, and once in awhile a red fox passes by. The warbler has never seen the two deer mice that

The black-throated blue warbler is a good example of why warblers are often called the "butter-flies" of the bird kingdom.

some nights scamper up the leafy slopes or the toads that chance by after the spring breeding season.

The warbler pauses in its hunt for insects to advertise its presence. "Zoo, zoo, zreeeee," it buzzes. An answering call comes from the male black-throated blue at the other end of the rise. At intervals the other bird repeats the song, but it never comes closer. This is correct and satisfactory. The first warbler drops down to a young maple and then to the ground. It picks insects from a rotting log lying next to the bleached, half-buried bones of a cow moose killed here by wolves three winters before. The warbler cocks its head to watch the broad-winged hawk on its nest, 30 feet up in the fork of a yellow birch. The hawk is incubating eggs and poses no immediate threat.

With a beakful of insects the warbler flies to another log, beside which, in a low fork of a small maple, there is a neat little bark-adorned nest. Inside, the brownish female broods four tiny, naked young birds. Their faint "cheeps" are temporarily stilled as their father thrusts insects down their gaping throats. Then he flies up, up into the green vault arching above his world.

Walking southwest on the Greenstone Trail, you enter the maple-birch forest near the top of Mount Desor. After the long open ridges and young birch forests, it is like going into a tunnel. The sun and the views are screened off. You are forced to look at things close at hand, or to retreat to your thoughts. On a hot day, the forest is a cool relief. On any day, it is an interesting change. Twelve miles down the trail, you finally emerge into the daylight near Windigo.

Maple-birch forest also covers much of Red Oak Ridge southwestward from Siskiwit Lake and some of Feldtmann Ridge. In future years it will probably reclaim several miles of Greenstone Ridge northeast from Mount Desor. This stretch, part of the 1936 burn area, is now covered with medium-sized birch and aspen, but underneath one sees thousands of small sugar maples awaiting their chance.

Sugar maple and yellow birch blanket Isle Royale's southwestern highlands.

In general, the maple-birch forest occupies the warmest, driest parts of Isle Royale; this means the highlands farthest above the cooling influence of Lake Superior. But within the total area of the forest are many variations in environment, which in turn produce variations in the forest.

Of the several tree species making up this forest type, each has its specific requirements. Sugar maple, the generally dominant species, occupies the warmest, driest areas, which also have fairly deep, well-drained soils. Altitude and southerly slopes provide the first conditions, glacial deposits the second. The tops of Mount Desor and Sugar Mountain have nearly pure stands of sugar maple. Here nature was apparently "helped" by Indians, who girdled other trees to encourage the sweet-sapped maples. Outward from here, other

95

species increasingly mix in. Yellow birch, the "second-in-command," needs somewhat more moisture, and its seedlings are somewhat less shade-tolerant than those of sugar maple. On lower parts of the ridges it shares dominance with sugar maple, and on Greenstone and Red Oak Ridges near Washington Harbor it takes over first place. White cedar, perhaps third in importance, can tolerate both wetness and dryness. Therefore it occurs throughout the maple-birch area, and in many swampy places it becomes the principal tree. White spruce and balsam fir, the ultimate presiding species on most of Isle Royale, occur sparingly through the maple-birch forest, mainly on north slopes and in dips in the southerly slopes, where moisture accumulates. This forest, then, is distinctly a hardwood, deciduous forest. Intensely green in summer, brilliant in fall, and skeletal in winter, it forms a striking contrast with the coniferous shoreline forests at the island's other environmental extreme.

Wherever sugar maple forms part of the overstory, it puts its structural stamp on the forest, as we saw on the warbler's knoll. It does this through prolific reproduction. So abundantly do its seeds germinate that the little maples often make a continuous cover over the ground, shading out most other plants. (The few herbaceous plants that do survive in these forests are mostly species found in other forest types as well—such as Canada dogwood, rosey twistedstalk, bluebead lily.) In areas where the canopy is closed, intercepting most of the sunlight, the maple seedlings remain small, waiting until the day a big tree falls, giving some a chance to grow. (Such blowdowns are rather infrequent, since trees here are better anchored and less susceptible to heart rot than those in the spruce-fir forest.) Where the canopy is more open, the young maples form an understory, vying with each other for ultimate positions in the overstory. In such a situation (again as on the warbler's knoll), the ground cover beneath the sapling maples is fairly sparse, though even here tiny maple seedlings manage to survive—a potential third wave, as it were. The maple's fantastic ability to reproduce is also demonstrated in some fringe areas, where scarcely a mature maple can be found. Going down the Greenstone Trail on the last long descent to Windigo, you see beneath the birches thickets of the irrepressible sugar maple.

With few conifers and only small amounts of combustible material near the ground, most of the maple-birch forest has escaped fire for a long time and has been able to reach maturity. For some animals that feed near the ground, this is a bad state of affairs. Deer mice find the pickings rather slim here. Hares, which need thick cover as well as low-growing plants to eat, generally are confined to the swampy coniferous pockets within the maple-birch area. Moose, though able to reach plenty of foliage, find little diversity in the menu.

This forest is much more generous to those animals that can reach its upper levels. Red squirrels can harvest maple and birch seeds and the many fungi that grow on old trees—trees that also offer them numerous nesting cavities. Birds, though perhaps less abundant and diverse here than in some of the other forest types, nevertheless occur in good numbers. Most of them feast on the insects that are feeding on the upper foliage. The great majority of birds escape the winter harshness by migrating south. Easily the most common are the ovenbird and red-eyed vireo. The ovenbird manages to find insects on the leafy forest floor, where it builds its domed nest. The red-eyed vireo hangs its little basket nest in the fork of an understory branch and feeds upward into the

Bird Monitoring and Biodiversity

▸● Human activities are rapidly reducing the variety of life on earth. As whole species and local populations of species go extinct, the economic benefits and ecological services those species provide are lost,

not to mention the joy we take in their presence. Such losses are occurring all over the earth, but especially in tropical forests, which harbor half or more of the world's species and are disappearing fast under the ax, saw, and fire. Isle Royale may seem remote from tropical forests, but many of the park's breeding birds winter in such forests. As these forests diminish, yearly surveys in North America show that many of our continent's breeding birds are also declining. Although changes on the breeding grounds may be partly responsible, losses of tropical forest wintering habitat are undoubtedly playing a part. ▸● In many national parks, monitoring of breeding bird populations is underway. A system for monitoring Isle Royale's breeding land birds was first developed and applied in 1994. All birds seen or heard are counted for ten minutes at points evenly spaced along six trails. These trails, widely scattered through Isle Royale, from Passage Island to Windigo, were selected to sample eight major land habitat types. Experienced birders made the counts in the last half of June, when all the birds found could be considered breeders and singing is at a peak. ▸● The counters recorded 1,008 individual birds of 56 species. The ten most common, in descending order, were ovenbird (108), Nashville warbler, white-throated sparrow, winter wren, red-eyed vireo, chestnut-sided warbler,

black-throated green warbler, American crow, Swainson's thrush, and magnolia warbler. At the other end of the scale, 11 species were represented by only one individual. Only two black-throated blue warblers, the species featured in this chapter, were counted. This bird, though still regular at the west end of Isle Royale, is declining in Michigan and may be having trouble on its wintering grounds. ►●

As these counts are made each year, significant declines or increases in populations will be noted. In protected natural areas like Isle Royale and other national parks, where major habitat types change very slowly from year to year, short of fire, a downward trend in a migratory species is likely to indicate problems on the wintering grounds or along the migration routes. Steps can then be taken to identify the problems and try to do something about them. ►●

canopy. You can hear its monotonous question-and-answer phrases all day long.

Considered now to be a relict of an earlier warm-dry period, when they were much more extensive, Isle Royale's maple-birch forests await the dictates of climatic change—expansion if the climate warms, extinction if it cools. Meanwhile they add pleasantly to the diversity of life and landscape on the island.

The Loon
INLAND LAKES

It is noon. The sun shines warmly on the quiet water of Siskiwit Lake, sprawling in its great depression between the Lake Superior shore and Greenstone Ridge. The forest enclosing it stands tall and green on the south side, where aspen and birch have had a century to grow since the last fire, and shorter and green on the north side, where the 1936 fire burned clear down the ridge to the lake. At either end, dark swamp conifers stretch back to other, smaller lakes. Circling high above the lake, gulls are moving dots of white.

Out near the middle of Siskiwit Lake, near Ryan Island, a loon dozes, bill tucked under his wing. Just off the shore of the island, his mate shepherds their two light brown young. Like all young loons, they had taken to the water the day they hatched, but they still depend on their parents for food.

Having rested enough, the male wakes up and dives. Soon after submerging, he spies whitefish and ciscos; they are too far away to be overtaken. He continues down, into the dim world a hundred feet beneath the surface. Here, just above the fine brown mud covering the bottom rock, he comes upon a lake trout. But it is too big. He angles up toward the light. On his way, a school of young ciscos flashes by. He spurts after them and catches one that lags. Continuing underwater, he swims to his family and breaks the surface with his prize. He mashes the cisco in his bill and passes it to his mate, who feeds it to one of the young.

As the male swims slowly away, six loons down the lake begin yodeling. Two pairs and two unmated birds have joined in a tight flock on the water and now circle around, calling crazily. The male, a mile away, wails in answer. With feet spattering and stiff wing-tips hitting the surface, he makes a long takeoff, then arcs over the middle of the lake, where the other loons have congregated. But the instinct to feed his family is stronger than the social pull of his brethren. He turns and flies back to the east end of the lake.

Here the rock bottom slopes up and stream deposits lie in quiet coves along the shore, making shallow water where aquatic plants can grow, small fish can thrive, and snails, mussels, and leeches can find food. Among the many little islands, female mergansers and goldeneyes lead their broods. Along the shore, teetering spotted sandpipers search for insects. Crowding down almost to the water, green alders, ninebark, sweet gale, and white cedar make a dense shoreline fringe.

The loon finds good feeding here in the shallows. Much of the afternoon he flies back and forth from these quiet coves to his family with offerings of snails, leeches, and small fish. A mink hunts here too, leaving empty mussel shells strewn along the shore. Among the horsetails, burreeds, spikerush, and yellow pond lilies, great long pike pursue smaller fish, seizing them in their saw-toothed jaws and gulping them into their cavernous mouths.

The hours pass. The sun turns red and sinks below Greenstone Ridge. Up in the birches on the north side of the lake, a hermit thrush salutes the evening with liquid, ethereal song. In a small cove behind a rocky peninsula, beavers emerge from their lodge and make V's through the water, intent on foraging. Two bats flutter erratically over the lake, catching insects. Off toward Wood Lake, a loon utters a long, gull-like cry, sending echoes ricocheting across the water. Then, as if set off by this sound, a pack of wolves somewhere on the south shore begins howling. Punctuated by yips and barks, the voices rise and fall, saying something that needs to be said.

The male loon patters across the water, lifts into the air, and disappears slowly toward Siskiwit Bay, his stiff wings "putt-putting" like some distant outboard.

*I*n some ways, Siskiwit Lake mirrors all the lakes of Isle Royale. It has the cold-water fish of the few deep lakes, and at its shallow ends it has much of the plant and animal life typical of the smaller, shallower lakes.

Of Isle Royale's 42 named lakes, four are oligotrophic; that is, they are cold, deep, and clear, and are poor in nutrients. In addition to Siskiwit, they are Desor, Sargent, and Richie. The first three have one or more forms of the cisco-whitefish group; Richie does not. Siskiwit Lake also has the cold-water lake trout, which fishermen pursue in summer by bumping baits along the bottom. These lakes, because of their low levels of nutrients, support only small numbers of plankton (microscopic plants and animals). The rocky bottoms are too deep for much sunlight to reach them, and most of the shore is unprotected from wave action; thus there are few places favorable to rooted aquatic plants. But on Siskiwit there are a few sheltered spots that meet their requirements.

All the island's other lakes are classed as eutrophic or dystrophic. They are characterized by shallow, warm water colored by organic matter and tannic acid; high nutrient levels; and abundant plankton and rooted aquatics. In these lakes, the balance is being tipped in favor of plant over animal life. Among the many plants that take root on the bottom and send shoots above the surface or below it are spikerush, burreed, yellow pond lily, horsetail, northern naiad, cattail, and various kinds of pondweed.

With less diversity of habitats present, there are fewer species of fish in shallow lakes than in the deeper lakes. The dominant predatory fish are northern pike and yellow perch. White sucker, blacknose and golden shiner, and brook stickleback are common plant-feeders. The redbelly dace, finescale dace, and fathead minnow are particularly typical of some of the shallower, more stagnant lakes, such as Lily, Wallace, and Sumner.

Lake Richie is classified as oligotrophic—cold, deep, and clear, while Moose Lake (opposite) is dystrophic—characterized by shallow warm water with high nutrient levels.

In the shallow, quiet water near lake shores you are also likely to find snails, mussels, and those friendless creatures, leeches, of which Isle Royale has about 15 species. Snails feed on algae growing on rocks. Mussels burrow part way into the sand or mud and siphon water, ingesting the copepods and other minute animals in it and pumping out the rest. Most leeches eat small animal life, such as insects up to about 1/4 inch. Some species of leech attach themselves to animals, including humans, and suck blood—which is why, when swimming in the inland lakes, you should check well for leeches upon leaving the water. One very small species fastens onto the gills of fish. Along the shore of any lake you are apt to surprise green frogs, the island's most common amphibian.

Several kinds of mammals and many birds that feed on aquatic life are found around the inland lakes. Moose are especially fond of aquatic plants, and beavers like them too.

Mink restlessly search out frogs, snakes, fish, birds, and other small animals, while their larger cousin, the otter, feeds chiefly on fish, pursuing them with marvelous, fluid speed. Muskrats, scarce on the island, feed mainly on plants but also eat mussels, other small aquatic animals, and carrion. On the larger lakes, red-breasted and common mergansers dive for fish, while goldeneye ducks may be found on almost any lake or beaver pond. Gulls keep an eye on all water bodies, and loons, which need a long run to lift their heavy bodies into the air, visit any lake with adequate takeoff space.

Along shores, great blue herons stalk fish and other aquatic animals, spotted sandpipers hunt at the water's edge, and kingfishers dive for small fish from overhanging branches or from the air. Occasionally, ospreys may be seen at inland lakes, where from high in the air they plunge into the water

A Loon's Life ⊸ Most Isle Royale loon chicks break out of their shells in June; but some, from late-nesting parents, hatch in July. For a month, they have developed in their egg under the brooding of their parents. When they peck their way out, they find themselves on a vegetation-lined nest at the edge of the water, often on a small island for protection

from predators. Their male parent has arrived in April or May, just after ice-out, and selected his territory. He has looked for one that has clear water for underwater visibility, a good supply of fish, a variety of bottom types and depths, and quiet, protected places in which to raise chicks. It also has, if possible, a nesting island with a steep drop-off for quick and inconspicuous arrival and departure from the nest and with a good view of the territory. The female parent has arrived soon after the male. If the territory is on a

small inland lake, the pair will own it alone; if it's on a large lake they probably will share the lake with other pairs, in separate territories. ⊸ Within 24 hours after hatching, the chicks enter the water with their parents, never to return to the nest. They swim with their parents to the nursery area, a sheltered place where they will remain the first two weeks and maybe longer. Constantly the parents must guard against herring gulls and large fish that might prey on the chicks. As the young grow and gradually learn to feed themselves, they travel with their parents over a larger area. Not until they are three months old, however, can they fully take care of themselves. ⊸ During late summer, adult loons leave their young occasionally to gather in social groups outside defended territories. They call, circle around, and dive, presumably preparing themselves for cooperative feeding during the migration to come. In August and September the adults gradually gather on the larger lakes and then migrate through the upper Great Lakes, mostly in September and October. The juveniles follow a similar pattern, but tend to migrate later. ►➤ Most common loons winter along the Atlantic, Pacific, and Gulf coasts in groups, although a few remain inland on ice-free waters. The juveniles are something of a mystery. It takes them three or four years to get the adult plumage and they remain in the ocean during this time, apparently moving northward in summer. It's not known at what age they breed. Loon researchers on Isle Royale have banded both adult and juvenile loons, attracting them at night with loon calls, spotlighting them to prevent their seeing the boat, and scooping them up in a salmon net. Perhaps recovery of banded juveniles on the ocean or upon return as adults to Isle Royale will help to clear up some of the mysteries about these wild spirits of the island. ►➤

for fish. Bald eagles, too, include inland lakes in their large territories. They take fish alive or dead, snatching them from the surface, and any other small animal life not agile enough to elude them.

Bald eagles and ospreys, formerly regular nesters on Isle Royale, were hard hit by DDT and other persistent pesticides used widely in the 1950s and 1960s. These chemicals accumulated in fish, the primary food of these birds, and caused thinning of their eggshells. By around 1970, successful rearing of young on Isle Royale apparently ceased. DDT and similar pesticides were banned in 1972, but it was not until 1984 that a successful osprey nest and 1985 that a successful eagle nest were observed on Isle Royale. Since that time, two or three pairs of ospreys have produced young most years, and eagles have gradually increased. In 1994

six active eagle nests fledged nine young. Ospreys and eagles build their big stick nests high up in trees, ospreys usually choosing dead trees while eagles use live ones. Some of the abandoned nests remain for years, slowly disintegrating.

Playful and social otters are efficient predators of fish in Isle Royale's inland lakes, pursuing them with marvelous, fluid speed.

The peregrine falcon suffered even more from pesticides, disappearing as a breeding bird in eastern United States. On Isle Royale, the last known peregrine nest was found in 1955. From 1987 to 1991, the park staff raised young peregrines on the island in hack boxes, with the hope that some would return as adults to nest. This practice has been successful elsewhere in North America, but as of 1994 no nesting had been reported on Isle Royale. Peregrines are seen here occasionally and suitable cliffs exist, so perhaps this regal bird will eventually nest here again.

Hard hit in the 1950s and 1960s by the use of DDT and other persistent pesticides, ospreys have made a remarkable comeback since 1984.

Three of Isle Royale's lakes have witnessed the evolution of new species or subspecies. Siskiwit Lake, although only fifty feet higher than Lake Superior, has been separated from it for about 5,000 years. In this time, through small mutations and differential survival of mutants, the ciscos in Siskiwit Lake have changed enough to be considered a new species. In Sargent Lake, about 100 feet above Lake Superior, a subspecies, the Sargent Lake cisco, has evolved. Lake Desor can make sole claim to two subspecies: the Lake Desor cisco and the Lake Desor whitefish. And Lake Harvey has three — a pearl dace, a blacknose shiner, and a fathead minnow — all bearing its name. In the case of each lake, isolation from Lake Superior and other inland lakes on the island prevented the intermixing of populations that would have kept them genetically uniform. Why *all* the species in these three lakes did not develop into new forms will probably remain one of the mysteries of evolution.

For all their specialized forms of life and apparent permanence, lakes are nevertheless one of the more ephemeral features of nature. They die partly through the downcutting of their outlets, which lowers the surface of the lake; but the chief agents of death are siltation and spreading plants. Wherever the water is shallow and quiet, aquatic plants take root. On the shallower lakes, a floating mat of vegetation may develop and eventually cover the surface. Water lilies, spikerushes, and others we have mentioned begin the process. As the vegetation becomes denser, trapping more and more silt and organic debris, sedges begin to form a mat on the surface. Gradually this sedge mat extends farther and farther out over the water, as dead plants and roots help to fill in the space underneath. As the shoreward parts of the mat fill in and become somewhat drier, sphagnum moss often begins growing on it. Whether sphagnum appears or not, shrubs soon become established; leatherleaf, bog rosemary, and alders are the most common. Where sphagnum is present, Labrador tea usually takes root, eventually choking out the other small shrubs and much of the sphagnum as well.

As the sedge mat continues to grow out over the lake, succession progresses on the landward parts. Debris from the plants helps to build soil, and certain trees become established. Where the soil is slightly acid, black spruce becomes the dominant species. Where it is slightly alkaline, white cedar is more prevalent. Sometimes a few tamaracks also grow in these bog forests.

Eventually, as the soil builds and dries, the climax species become established. Since most lakes and bogs on Isle Royale are at the lower elevations, these species usually will be white spruce and balsam fir. When this stage is reached, after many human lifetimes, all influence of the former lake is gone. It is truly dead.

On Isle Royale you can see all phases of lake extinction.

Hidden Lake, for instance, at the start of the Lookout Louise Trail, has an irregular fringe of bog mat. Lily Lake, in the southwest part of the island, is half closed over with a classic floating mat. Walking on it you can feel it spring up and down. Growing on the spongy surface are specialized plants such as sundew, pitcher-plant, and certain orchids, such as grass pink and ladies' tresses. At Raspberry Bog, on Raspberry Island, the mat has closed completely. A boardwalk nature trail here takes you through successive zones—from black spruce to Labrador tea to leatherleaf—that represent phases in formation of the bog. And looking down from almost any ridge, you can see dark conifer swamps. Some of these may stand in

place of former lakes. You are witness to yet another aspect of change on ever-changing Isle Royale.

Cow lilies bloom in shallow lake waters; they are precursors to denser vegetation.

Some lakes, however, will resist a very long time. The larger and deeper a lake, the longer it will take to fill. Depth is an obvious deterrent, but large surface size slows the filling process in less obvious ways. Over lakes such as Siskiwit, Desor, and Feldtmann, the winds sweep unobstructed, building up large waves. These discourage establishment of aquatic vegetation. And during warm spells in winter, the ice cover expands, pushing out over the shore and bulldozing anything in its way.

Ten thousand years from now—to be optimistic in more than one way—our descendants may still hear loons wailing on the broad waters of Siskiwit Lake.

The Beaver
PONDS AND STREAMS

*I*t is late summer, 1973. The trail crew doesn't know it, but they have helped the beavers. Alongside the trail leading into Chippewa Harbor the beavers have created ponds. Some of the aspens they cut fell across the trail, and the trail crew has had to saw off the blocking trunks and branches. This has saved the beavers a lot of work. Now they are simply dragging the branches to their pond and consuming the tender parts. Floating in the water near shore, each beaver takes the small end of a branch in its front paws and feeds it into its mouth. "Crunch, crunch, crunch"—the next piece gets processed.

This beaver family—father and mother with last year's and this year's young—indeed have been living amidst plenty. In the past few years they have worked down along a small stream, building a succession of ponds between two low rocky ridges crowned with jack pine. Their current lodge is in the middle of the last pond, secure from invasion. From this lodge they can travel up through their six ponds, in summer harvesting mostly herbaceous plants and thimbleberries on shore, and in spring and fall any of the numerous aspens and birches that grow in the surrounding forest. Up to a point, that is, for the farther they venture from the water the more vulnerable they become—each foot of distance from the safety of a pond increases the chance that a wandering wolf might catch them. Thus far, with plenty of trees left, they have cut no farther than 100 feet from shore. At the head of the uppermost pond, however, they have dug a channel 150 feet long to allow them to reach some particularly big aspens.

Beaver ponds afford some of the best wildlife watching on Isle Royale.

With many aspens—their favorite food—and many birches around, the beavers have been wasteful. Inevitably, some of the cut trees lodged against their neighbors, but even on trees that fell to the ground, many accessible branches have not been used. The beavers cannot afford this profligacy for very long, because they have reached the dammable limits of the stream. It trickles through their lowermost dam, across the trail, and down a steep hillside. Upstream from their six active ponds, they or their ancestors have already exploited the forest, leaving a series of old grassy ponds and wet meadows. Some birches but few aspens remain in those areas.

As the beavers chew aspen branches this rainy afternoon in late July, other creatures are also using the pond the beavers have made. Like knots on old logs that lie in the water, gray-brown goldeneyes and hooded mergansers sit motionless. Now half-grown, they have known no other world than these ponds, criss-crossed with fallen trees and the white reflections of still-standing birches killed by the water. On other logs, painted turtles rest like stones. In the leaf-filled shal-

lows along shore, green frogs, too, sit still. But some creatures, like the beavers, are on the move. Garter snakes crawl slowly along the pond edge, hunting frogs. A muskrat swims away with some of the beavers' aspen twigs. A solitary sandpiper, resting at the pond in its late-summer migration south, flutters up with a sharp "peet-weet!" as the muskrat passes. Between the two rock ridges flanking the ponds fly birds of the forest — blue jays, gray jays, woodpeckers, chickadees. The pond is indeed a focus of life.

The beaver, creating a new environment wherever it goes, has a great ecological impact on this island.

As afternoon becomes evening, a cow moose wanders over the ridge with her calf. From the opposite direction — up the hill from Chippewa Harbor — comes a spike-horn bull, his one-pronged little antlers fuzzy with velvet. He sloshes through the upper ponds, being careful to avoid the cow. But now all the moose freeze. They have heard a deep bark from down on the trail to Lake Mason. Silently they melt back into the forest. A few minutes later the gray forms of wolves appear at the pond's edge. They sniff along and they listen for the sound of a beaver chewing. But all the beavers are in the pond. The wolves lap at the water, then trot up the trail toward Lake Richie. Their hunt has just begun. Slowly, pausing often to test the air, the parent beavers swim toward shore to begin the night's harvest.

*O*n Isle Royale, wherever there is water deep enough to dive in, or a trickle that can be dammed, there are likely to be beavers. When populations are high, they inhabit protected Lake Superior shorelines, most inland lakes, and a multitude of ponds of their own making. But beaver populations, like those of most mammals on Isle Royale, go decidedly up and down. In the nineteenth century, beavers were virtually trapped out of Isle Royale. Numbers rose in this century but fell again in the 1940s and 1950s, presumably because of an epizootic disease such as tularemia. Aerial beaver counts begun in 1962 showed a rise to around 1,900 animals in 1974, then a crash to about 600 in 1980, probably because of record high wolf numbers. As many of the wolves themselves died off, beavers again increased to another peak in 1986. Then, once again, the pendulum swung the other way, this time, perhaps, because food supplies were diminishing. Many aspens and birches had grown old and died, moose browsing on the reproduction of these trees had been heavy, and the beavers themselves had cut many of the food trees within safe reach of their ponds. Still, beavers continued to be a major factor in the island's ecology.

No other animal, in fact, including the moose, has as much ecological effect on Isle Royale as the beaver, for this big rodent creates a new environment wherever it goes. When beavers enter virgin territory to build a dam, they kill a section of forest by flooding. This drives out terrestrial animals and most of those inhabiting the trees. Around the shores of the ponds they open the forest further by cutting shrubs and trees, particularly aspen and birch.

While the beavers are destroying forest habitat, to the detriment of some animals, they are creating new habitat for others. The environment for such quiet-water fish as white suckers, brook sticklebacks, golden shiners, and blacknose shiners is greatly expanded. Frogs and painted turtles find new territory, while frog hunters such as garter snakes and minks are given new hunting grounds.

Beaver ponds afford some of the best wildlife watching on the island. Creep up to any pond, sit quietly, and you are bound to see something interesting. Maybe it will be a moose, come for aquatic plants. Perhaps you will see the makers of the pond themselves, eating, grooming, or working on their dam or lodge. And

Beaver ponds provide moose with mineral-rich plants they can find nowhere else.

always there will be birds about. If you have arrived stealthily, you may get good looks at mallards, black ducks, teal, goldeneyes, hooded mergansers, or ring-necked ducks. In the first half of summer there probably will be tree swallows, coming and going from their woodpecker-hole nests in dead trees. A kingfisher or great blue heron might be fishing there. Watch for cedar waxwings, king-birds, or olive-sided flycatchers snatching insects from the air over the pond. And listen for song sparrows and swamp sparrows singing from the marshy fringes.

Each beaver pond is different, not only in its activity at any given moment, but also in its situation and appearance. If the valley is deep and narrow, the pond will be deep and narrow, as was the case of the ponds described near Chip-pewa Harbor. If the valley is broad, with gentle slopes, the pond will be shallow, with much vegetation. If the pond is fairly new, it will probably have many dead trees or even some live ones standing in it; older ponds will be more open. A new pond created at an old pond site, where a meadow had developed, may be dotted with islands of grass and sedge. Some ponds are large; others are small. On a tiny rivulet I saw one that was five feet wide and eight feet long—a useless monument to the beaver's eternal dam-building urge.

When a beaver colony exhausts the food supply at its pond, it moves to a new site, allowing a reclamation process to begin at the old one. Without attention, breaks in the dam allow the pond to drain, leaving a bare, muddy surface. This is soon invaded by annuals and short-lived perennials, such as touch-me-nots, loosestrife, joe-pye weed, raspberry, sedges, and rushes. These gradually give way to bluejoint grass, which covers not only the old pond bottom but also the remains of the dam and lodge. Very slowly, speckled alder extends its control from the edges toward the center. In these early stages of succession, red-winged blackbirds, swamp and song spar-rows, and sedge wrens are given new nesting areas. After many years, if another beaver colony does not occupy the site, the surrounding forest may succeed in reclaiming its former territory. This last phase is exceedingly slow, however, because the dense cover of grass and shrubs, as well as adverse chemical conditions in the soil, discourages tree establishment. Thus, beavers may be viewed as agents of diversification, working against the forest's trend toward uniformity.

By 1994, the beaver ponds described at the beginning of this chapter had been abandoned and were starting the process described above. The outlet stream had cut through the dam and sedges, grasses, joe-pye weed, goldenrod, and other plants made a meadow where water had once stood. No aspens remained along the trail. The beavers had moved or died.

Of all the beaver's relationships with other animals, perhaps most important ecologically are those with the moose; and the moose gets much the better of it. The ponds provide moose with aquatic plants, which contain minerals they can't get elsewhere. But each bite taken by moose means several less for beavers, which also like aquatic plants. By cutting aspens and birches, beavers provide moose with tree-top foliage and bark they could not otherwise reach and with root sprouts sent up by the cut trees. So intense is the browsing, and so great is the competition from shrubs and conifers, that most of the resprouting aspens are killed, thus depriving beavers of a new supply of their primary food source.

The streams of Isle Royale, which offer beavers so many possibilities for ponds, constitute in themselves yet another type of environment. Sluggish streams, particularly those flowing through meadows or marshes, have much the same kinds of life, though less of it, that beaver ponds have. The more rapid streams harbor sculpins, white suckers, longnose dace, and sometimes brook or rainbow trout. Washington and Grace Creeks have both resident and spawning trout. The Little Siskiwit River is also known for its brook trout. In the spring, smelt and thousands of white suckers run up many streams to spawn.

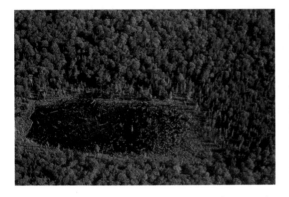

When a beaver colony exhausts the food supply at its pond, it moves to a new site on the island.

Most of the water draining off Isle Royale first flows quickly in little brooks down ridge slopes, then turns sluggish as it reaches valleys and drains through swamps and beaver ponds toward Lake Superior. Waterfalls are few, those on the Little Siskiwit River and Siskiwit Lake outlet being among the better known ones.

Oddly enough, at the mouths of some Isle Royale streams that empty into long harbors or bays, the flow alternates between downstream and upstream. In most of these cases, the flow shifts direction every 10 to 30 minutes. This phenomenon is not well understood, but it is not tidal. It is thought to be caused by the periodic building up and release of water at the heads of the harbors. Wind, if it is blowing up-harbor, and stream discharge cause the water to build up. Periodically, the build-up becomes great enough to cause a down-harbor shift, thus allowing the stream to flow in its normal direction. Washington and Tobin Creeks and the Big Siskiwit River exhibit this phenomenon quite markedly. Over Lake Superior as a whole, differences in atmospheric pressure cause similar, though less regular, effects. Such oscillating waves, known as seiches, occur in many lakes, bays, and gulfs of the world.

As we have seen, the watery lowlands of Isle Royale provide for the needs of many forms of life. Let's climb now to a very different sort of place, where heat, dryness, wind, and lack of trees call for different strategies by other kinds of creatures.

Counting Beavers ◦► Estimating populations of wild animals is seldom easy. If you're relying on counts of seen animals, you're never entirely sure how many you didn't see; and if you're using secondary evidence, like tracks or scats, the results are even less certain. In many cases, the counts can only indicate trends,

not total numbers. On Isle Royale, trends in snowshoe hare populations have been deduced from the number seen per 100 kilometers hiked in summer, and trends in red fox numbers from aircraft observations in winter. Total counts of wolves, thought to be exact or nearly exact, and counts of moose have also been made from the air in winter. ◦► Counting beavers is a two-part process. Active colonies are identified and mapped from the air, and the number of beavers per colony must be determined by other means. On Isle Royale ten counts were made between 1962 and

1992. Most were conducted by Philip Shelton, one of the Purdue University graduate students doing research under Durward Allen. Phil made the 1962 aerial count in October, after most leaves were off the trees, along with a moose count. The pilot flew at 500 to 600 feet along parallel strips while Phil recorded fresh food piles underwater at beaver lodges, which indicated active colonies.  To get an estimate of the number of beavers per colony, along with other information, Phil live-trapped beavers at a number of colonies over a three-year period. Using the ratio of known adults (two per colony) to the number of trapped adults, and applying this ratio to the young as well, he arrived at an average of 6.4 beavers per colony, a number used in all subsequent beaver counts. He obtained his estimates of beaver populations by multiplying the average number of beavers per colony by the total number of observed colonies. Essentially the same method for estimating beavers has been used in the later counts, with the addition of two beavers per site where signs were noted but no food pile. There is a question, however, whether the 6.4 beavers per colony is still valid after 30 years of change—another example of the difficulty of estimating wildlife populations.

The Kestrel
OPEN RIDGES

BRIAN E. SMALL / VIREO

*E*ven at 6 o'clock this early August morning, the sun is hot on Green-stone Ridge. Rising red above Lake Supe-rior, it sends its rays unopposed against the open, rocky slopes, further drying the grasses and slowing the activity of animals.

But though it is hot on the open ridge east of Mt. Ojibway, there is some action. Perched in a hazelnut thicket, a song sparrow sings. In another thicket, a red squirrel rustles, search-ing for curve-beaked hazelnuts. On the Greenstone Trail between two thickets a snowshoe hare nips wild strawberry leaves. Far down the slope, a red fox picks its way between the shrubs, alert for hare, bird, or mouse; if unsuccessful, it will descend into the forest for wild sarsaparilla berries—a never-failing resource this time of year.

At the tip of a dark spruce tree, a young kestrel perches awkwardly, crying for food. But the hawk's parents are busy hunting. The trim female sits on the limb of a dead aspen, studying the ground. Her sharp eyes scan the rocks, gray-green with lichens and crevice-lined with grass and bush honeysuckle. Out of the gray-green-brown background she discerns an interesting shape. She plummets to the rock and seizes a grasshopper in her talons, then returns to her perch. Seeing all this, the young bird flutters to the aspen, but approaching the limb too fast can't hold on and pitches forward. It circles around, and on the second try manages to land. The mother bird rewards it with a mangled grasshopper.

The male kestrel cruises above the ridge toward the fire tower, now flapping, now gliding, now hovering to inspect something below. He sees many things, but not all are significant to him. In a thicket of red maple, juneberry, and hazelnut a dark brown shape resolves into a bull moose intent on getting a last few mouthfuls before the heat drives him down into the forest. Across the trail, an oval depression remains in the grass where the bull slept part of the night. Briefly, the kestrel slows in his flight as he passes over a family of flickers stabbing the ground for ants, a cedar waxwing flycatching in the air, a robin caroling one last time this morning. But these are all too big for the little falcon. He speeds on, searching for a sparrow, warbler, grasshopper, deer mouse, or red-bellied snake.

Then a dark shadow crosses the ground. The kestrel

looks up, climbs, then dives on the much larger red-tailed hawk. The redtail evades the rush and hastens on, eager to be free of its small tormentor. The kestrel pursues it as far as the fire tower, then turns and glides back toward his family. The sun highlights the reds and blues on his back and wings.

Far out and below the sun, white cottony fog creeps across the surface of the lake. Soon it will envelop the island, blotting out the ridges and valleys, the lakes, the forest. Today fog, tomorrow wind, next week a storm will interrupt the heat that prevails on the summer ridges.

*T*his piece of Greenstone Ridge is one of the larger open areas on Isle Royale. Similar openings occur on other parts of Greenstone Ridge and on Minong and Feldtmann Ridges, with small patches scattered elsewhere. Generally, these nonforested strips are the result of fire aided by erosion and drought. Ridgetops, being the highest land on the island, frequently are hit by lightning, which sometimes starts fires. After a fire, the denuded soil is easily eroded. On any slope, erosion continually occurs on a small scale, but the lower parts also continually receive soil from upslope. On a ridgetop, of course, there is no higher source. Here, creation of new soil must proceed faster than erosion in order to make any headway. Organic debris is the principal building material of soil on ridges, but vegetation is discouraged by the thinness of the soils and the dryness caused by steep slopes, sun-heating, and wind. If plant succession does proceed toward forest, fire promoted by the dryness may at any time set it back. Thus, the ecological dog has itself by the tail, and some stretches of ridgetop may remain open for decades or even centuries.

The plant life on open ridgetops is mainly that charac-

teristic of early stages of succession. Such places are usually a patchwork of bare rock, grassy areas with small shrubs such as blueberry and bush honeysuckle,

Ridgetops often remain open for decades or more due to fire aided by erosion and drought.

shrubby thickets of hazelnut, juneberry, and sometimes young red and sugar maples, and scattered trees representative of the surrounding forest.

The animal life is also distinctive, and some species are restricted to such open areas. The larger animals are those found throughout the island. Moose most often visit the open ridges in early spring, when some herbaceous plants are sprouting and two favored shrubs, hazelnut and juneberry, are leafing. Hares enjoy the abundant low growth throughout the year but particularly in the green seasons. Wolves take advantage of the easy traveling on ridges, turning aside when a moose is started. Red foxes hunt fruits as well as animal prey. Red squirrels sometimes visit the thickets, apparently for their seeds and fruits.

On the other hand, many of the birds of open ridges are generally restricted to this type of habitat. Kestrels, which

rely heavily on large insects such as grasshoppers, are typical inhabitants, often nesting in old flicker holes in dead trees. Chipping sparrows, bluebirds, starlings, robins, cedar waxwings, and chestnut-sided, mourning, and Nashville warblers also favor this kind of environment.

Sharp-tailed grouse choose open grassy areas for their showy courtship dances, but they haven't been seen for several years, and may now be extinct.

Isle Royale's ridgetops thus offer the hiker the opportunity to explore a distinctive environment in all stages of plant succession from bare rock to mature forest. He or she will enjoy wild strawberries in early summer and blueberries in late summer, as well as incomparable views of the island, the big lake, and the mainland hills, and will experience the ever-changing weather that presides over all.

Ups and Downs of the Sharp-Tailed Grouse

➤● "I shot 3 prairie chickens on the Island today," wrote John Malone in the Menagerie Island Light Station journal for October 7, 1888. These "prairie chickens" were sharp-tailed grouse, a species seen by numerous island residents and scientists around the turn of the century. In 1986, researcher Chris Martin could find no sharp-tailed grouse on the island. ➤● What had happened to the grouse? Essentially, most of their habitat had disappeared. Martin reconstructed the story as follows. In the late nineteenth century, miners and loggers burned or cleared large areas of Isle Royale, creating expanses of grassy and brushy land, good habitat for sharp-tailed grouse. Sometime probably during the nineteenth century sharp-tailed grouse arrived on Isle Royale. No record exists of stocking by islanders, so the birds must have flown from the Canadian shore, alternately sailing and beating their short, rounded wings. Ruffed and spruce grouse, weaker fliers, never got here. ➤● From then up to the 1950s, most of the sharp-tailed grouse sightings were made in the Lake Siskiwit-Feldtmann Ridge area, where nineteenth century clearing was augmented by the 1936 fires. But as forest reclaimed the burned areas, sharp-tails disappeared from them. After the 1950s, sharp-tails were seen mostly in the remaining open areas of Greenstone Ridge, around Mt. Siskiwit and in the Mt. Ojibway–Mt. Franklin openings. As these open areas gradually contracted and grassy spots suitable for the grouse's dancing ground disappeared, the population dwindled. Today the sharp-tailed grouse is gone or nearly gone from the island. ➤● Will it return? Only the advent of sizable fires on Isle Royale and the presence of adventurous sharp-tails on the Canadian mainland is likely to make that possible. ➤●

The Time of Testing

Snow. Ice. Wind. Birches bare lines against the sky. Conifers green and full on the white hills. Silence. Now wind again. Hare tracks frozen across the trail. This is winter, the time of testing.

Bringing cold, wind, snow, and reduced food and cover, winter is indeed the most critical time of year for life on Isle Royale. But the island's plants and animals have a long time to prepare for it, since the slow-cooling water of Lake Superior warms the cold air above it until ice forms on the lake.

Fall may be considered to begin in August, when island birds begin migrating, and to end in November, when snow usually falls in earnest. In mid-September, maple leaves start turning red and yellow, and birches add their gold. Colors peak early in October as aspens, too, turn yellow. Then, with the first good wind, leaves fall. In October, brook trout, lake trout, and whitefish spawn. Moose, too, end the year with reproductive activity. The bulls have been getting more and more edgy since early September. They rub the velvet off their antlers in early September and track down cows through late September and October. Their calls and grunts resound through the fall forest, as do the bawls of the cows.

Meanwhile, insect numbers have been diminishing

rapidly. Mosquitoes have died out during August, flies in September. Most other insects are killed or go into hibernation during the frosts of September and October. Monarch butterflies, however, flutter south across Lake Superior toward Mexico, obeying the yearly command that pulses through their tiny nervous systems.

The camouflage white coat of the showshoe hare begins to make its dramatic appearance in late fall.

By late November, when the white winter blanket has settled, plants are dormant; insects, reptiles, and amphibians are hibernating; and most birds have migrated. Most of the mammal contingent, however, faces winter head on.

Of Isle Royale's current 15 species of mammals, only the bats hibernate or migrate to the south. To survive the winter, all others must find food and must themselves avoid becoming food for something else. Of Isle Royale's 120 or so species of summer birds, however, only about 20, joined by a few species from the Arctic, stay through the winter. These few birds and mammals are all that remains to enliven the elemental scene at this difficult time of year.

The conditions these animals must face vary from winter to winter, but always they are severe. Temperatures usually range between $-25°F$ and $+40°$. Frequent strong winds, generally from the west, add greatly to the chill of low temperatures. Snow depths range from one to three feet, with less under dense conifers and considerably more in drifts. Crust conditions within or on the snow sometimes help but more often hinder animals. Taken together, these conditions make great demands on the energy of animals, at a time when food is in shortest supply.

Over millennia, northern wildlife has evolved various strategies for survival. Birds, with the power of flight, can go long distances to find food. In winter, when birch seed is abundant, redpolls, pine siskins, and goldfinches may remain on the island in large numbers. In poor years they may wander in search of more productive areas. The same strategy is used by other northern finches, such as pine and evening grosbeaks, purple finches, and crossbills, depending on the supply of mountain-ash fruits, pine seeds, and other food.

Pine siskins may remain on the island in winter if birch seeds are abundant; relying on insect eggs and larvae, the blue jay (opposite) is a predictable year-round resident.

Birds that rely more on insect eggs and larvae—such as chickadees, blue and gray jays, and woodpeckers—have a more dependable source and consequently remain on the island in fairly stable numbers from one winter to another. Along the south shore, where the lake is usually open, a few mergansers and goldeneyes sometimes gather to feed on fish and other aquatic life. The ducks thus hunt in an environment that is usually considerably warmer than the air above. A few birds of prey, such as goshawks, horned owls, and in some years snowy owls from the Arctic find enough birds and small mammals to tide them over.

Plant-eating mammals, which are prey species, have developed highly individualistic methods for coping with winter and its predators. Deer mice and red squirrels lay up provisions during the long fall in numerous caches—in trees, logs, or underground. Mice and squirrels store mostly seeds of various kinds, though squirrels may rely on fungi and birch and alder catkins in years when conifer seeds are scarce. For these little animals, the snow is a blessing, providing them with covered runways hidden from most predators and with insulation from the chill air above.

Beavers have a winter system of living that insulates them almost completely from atmospheric rigors and the danger of predators. Before ice forms, they cut branches of aspen, birch, and other favored foods and stick them into or weight them with stones on the bottom of their pond or lake, usually near the lodge. They plaster their lodge with a new layer of mud, leaves, and sticks. When winter's cold spreads a layer of ice over the water and freezes the mud on its house, the beaver is effectively sealed in, and winter and predators are sealed out. When hungry, it leaves its lodge through an underwater entrance and visits the food cache. Occasionally, however, the beaver may leave the confines of home and pond to gnaw the bark from a tree felled in the fall. At such times it risks being caught by a wolf, perhaps a half-starved lone wolf rejected by the pack and unable to kill moose.

Muskrats lead a much more hazardous life. They do not store food for the winter, and though they feed upon aquatic plants and some animals beneath the ice, they also venture out for land plants. While foraging, they are under threat from virtually every predator on Isle Royale—mink, otter, weasel, red fox, wolf, and large hawks and owls. Perhaps it is only its caution and unspecialized food tastes that allow any muskrat to survive the winter.

Cover is surely the prime winter concern of the snow-shoe hare, for in most areas the supply of woody stems and twigs is adequate for its dietary needs. When winter strips away the deciduous leaves and green ground cover, the hare cannot safely wander as far as it did in summer. White-cedar swamps become headquarters for many hares, since they provide dense, low foliage that can also be eaten. On Isle Royale the hare's chief enemy is the red fox; the lynx, its principal predator through much of the north, rarely visits the island; and the wolves concentrate on moose. Hares rely on their speed and their broad, snowshoe feet to escape foxes. If the snow is soft, foxes will sink in farther than hares during a chase, but if a crust has formed the chase is more even. Its change in winter to a camouflaging white coat also aids the hare in its struggle to survive.

And what about the moose, that huge beast that eats more and provides more food for predators and scavengers than any other animal on the island? Snow depth seems to be the moose's main concern, since it affects ease of travel. During winters with deep snow, moose concentrate near shore-lines, where the abundant conifers intercept much of the falling snow and also provide browse. In these forests moose can also feed on twigs and bark of aspen, birch, and moun-tain-ash—among their favored foods. Frequent blowdowns put more food within reach. Deep, soft snow is more easily navigated by adult moose than by wolves, though calves are seriously hindered. A crust on or within the snow probably aids pursuing wolves. It seems, then, that food sources and snow depth regulate the moose's winter wandering, and that wolves are accepted as an environmental hazard. Healthy adult moose, in fact, seldom need to fear wolves; calves and infirm adults are the usual victims.

Predators, too, are faced by a reduced food supply in winter. Insects, reptiles, amphibians, and many birds have died, hibernated, or gone south. The young of various mam-

mals are not as abundant as in summer, having been reduced by the many hazards of their environment. The remaining prey animals spend more time in dens. Most predators, therefore, are forced to hunt farther and longer for a meal. The island's otters, for instance, must follow streams for miles, diving in

For the red fox winter is the critical season for survival on Isle Royale.

where fast water keeps ice from forming, and searching for fish and crustaceans as far under the ice as their lungs will allow.

In winter, red foxes have no easy job catching hares in the snow. In years of good mountain-ash crops, foxes, as well as ravens and other wildlife, eat many clusters of the orange-red fruit. As we will see shortly, foxes are also inadvertently assisted through the winter by wolves.

The wolf's only significant source of food in winter is the moose herd. Hares and smaller animals are hardly big enough to justify the energy expended in catching them, and beavers seldom venture ashore in that season. Possibly, wolves have an easier time finding and killing moose in winter than in any other season. Wolf packs hunt by following the easiest routes—usually on the windswept ice along shorelines, but sometimes inland along previously used routes. The wolves trot along, generally in single file, until moose or fresh tracks are found. If a discovered moose stands its ground they usually soon leave, wary of the animal's dangerous hooves. If the quarry runs, they chase it, single file. If deep snow, thick cover, or a long head start prevents them from catching up with the moose in a short time, they usually abandon the pursuit. But somehow they recognize weakness and keep after infirm individuals. Attacking mainly the rump, they slow the animal down, eventually bring it to the ground, and then quickly kill it. Some victims, however, are merely wounded and left to weaken and are killed later. After a kill, the wolves gorge, rest, then usually feed intermittently until the last bones are gnawed. A day or two after killing a calf, or several days after killing an adult, they are on the move again, seeking more fuel for their ever-burning bodily furnaces.

Wolves may have an easier time hunting moose in winter.

A kill has ecological importance that goes far beyond the survival of wolves. For when wolves leave a carcass, temporarily or permanently, other animals come for a share. Red

foxes, particularly, congregate at a kill, for the moment forgetting their territorial animosities. Ravens, it seems, make most of their winter livelihood from wolves. They actually follow wolf packs on the daily rounds, picking some sustenance from feces left by the wolves, and waiting for them to make a kill, from which they later get a meal or two. Gray jays and blue jays, smaller cousins of the raven, also visit moose carcasses for scraps. Tiny chickadees pick at the bone marrow where the opening is too small for ravens or jays. Deer mice undoubtedly gnaw the bone marrow, and red squirrels may sometimes make use of the kill. Any bald eagle that overwinters on the island is likely to take advantage of this free banquet, too. Thus several kinds of animals ride through winter partly on the coattails of the wolf.

In years of heavy winter snowfall, shoreline ice provides the easiest route for many animals including man.

Just as fall is prolonged by the warming effects of Lake Superior, so spring is delayed by the water's slow adjustment to the temperature of the air above. The patches and solid sheets of ice that form on much of the lake are slow to break up. When they finally do, the cold water continues to cool the spring air masses flowing over the lake. The shore ice usually goes in April, although some years it persists until May. On May 3, 1972, when *Ranger III* made its first trip of the year, it had to break ice in Rock Harbor for several hours before it could reach Mott Island. That day the snow lay 5 to 8 feet deep behind the park headquarters building.

During May, tree leaves begin unfurling; skunk cabbage, hepatica, and other early flowers bloom; smelt and suckers swarm up streams to spawn; birds return *en masse* from the south. By mid-June, when the trees are usually fully leaved and many forest flowers are blooming, summer can finally be acknowledged.

A Tale of Two Alphas ► We can only guess at the emotions of wild animals, but sometimes their behavior suggests that their feelings are very like our own. Rolf Peterson tells this story in his report on the 1993–94 Isle Royale wolf studies. ► "They became known to us, casually, as the 'Old Man' and the 'Old Lady,' the alpha pair of the Middle Pack. She was old, graying around her muzzle and sides, and she may have had other mates earlier in her life. When these two wolves paired off and claimed a territory in the middle of Isle Royale in 1990, they were the best hope for renewed reproduction. Their territory, dominated by mature birch, had very few moose, and wolf packs had not done well there since the 1970s. In August 1991 we radiocollared the male, but we found no evidence of reproduction that year. In 1992 we diligently monitored his radio signals in summer, and again failed to locate any pups. ► "By 1993 there was little hope that the Middle Pack would amount to much, and monitoring efforts were shifted to the other two packs. So it was a genuine surprise to find six wolves in the Middle Pack in January 1994, including four new pups! The alpha male's collar was in mortality mode, however, and we soon recovered his emaciated carcass. With severely worn teeth, he had simply run out of energy when the temperature bottomed out at − 36°C. ► "The male had wandered away from his pack before he died and, after waiting nearby on a kill for 10 days, the female led her four offspring on an extensive route through their territory, perhaps looking for her mate. Eighty kilometers later, the troupe ended up back on their kill, without ever finding the male (by then in our freezer). We wondered about the new burden on the female, having to kill moose without much assistance. As luck would have it, she led the pack outside their territory and found a moose that had fallen to its death off a north shore cliff, and it was here that we last observed the female alive, on February 7, 1994. We searched her territory in vain for a week without finding a trace of her. ►● "For three weeks the four pups relaxed together on the north shore, eating a second and then a third moose that fell off the north shore cliffs. They made one quick foray back into Middle Pack range and then returned to finish off the carcasses along the shore. ►● "On our last flight of the winter study, we found a fresh fox track along the shore almost 20 kilometers from the pups. We landed and followed the fox tracks onshore, and we were stunned to find the old female dead, sprawled on her chest beneath a spruce tree. She had continued to travel as long as she could and, like her mate, was emaciated with heavily-worn teeth. On their one trip 'home' the pups had come within a few meters of their dead mother, and they probably knew she was gone. ►● "This is not the way wolf societies usually work, as alpha wolves tend to feed themselves first and should outlast other pack members, even their own offspring. This alpha pair had been chronically undernourished for months, judging from weight-loss, and coincidentally each neared its end-point after they successfully raised their first litter of pups. The male, with an enlarged heart and a bruised liver, may have been pushed beyond the point of survival by record-low temperatures. And the female, gone a month later—what finally triggered her death? Coincidence, perhaps, but could it have been the death of her spouse? Ernest T. Seton, in 1894, caught a male wolf in New Mexico that had returned to where his mate had been killed a few days earlier. Seton chained the male overnight, but the wolf, with no apparent injury, was dead the following morning. Seton thought distress over the death of his mate triggered the male's own death. Such effects are well documented in our own species." ►●

Wolves, Moose, and the
Balance of Nature

*T*hrough the cycle of the seasons, and over decades and millennia, this tree-clothed rock we call Isle Royale has experienced and still experiences change of great magnitude. Between seasons, whole populations of plants and animals come or go or change their mode of existence. Over years, fire and wind unpredictably strike, for a while drastically altering the face of the landscape; and populations of living things fluctuate, sometimes violently. Over centuries, slow climatic change brings new assortments of plants and animals. Yet the island remains a green place teeming with life, and the diversity of life on it perhaps continues to grow. How does all this individual change result in a collective stability, and can we find in this ecological drama some lessons for our own species?

The now-famous story of the island's wolves and moose can begin to show us how the Isle Royale web of life hangs together. Sometime in the first decade of this century, it seems, moose became established (or reestablished) on the island. This significant happening was probably related to a regional change in the vegetation. Between 1890 and 1910, logging and fires in the northern Great Lakes area destroyed much of the reindeer lichen, on which caribou heavily depend, and created open areas where tree seedlings and shrubs—food for deer and moose—could flourish. Consequently, caribou decreased and deer and moose increased. Isle Royale's moose immigrants, which probably swam singly

The arrival of the gray wolf on Isle Royale in 1948–49 greatly moderated the catastrophic boom-and-bust cycle in the resident moose population.

or in small groups from the Canadian mainland, were perhaps pressured by a growing population to seek new feeding grounds. As sometimes happens when a new species reaches an island with suitable habitat and no natural predators, an

irruption followed. By 1930, when Adolph Murie studied the situation, the moose population had reached an estimated 1,000 to 3,000 animals, and a large part of the woody vegetation within

their reach was overbrowsed. Murie correctly predicted that starvation and disease would soon decimate the herd.

The first large die-off occurred in the winter of 1933. By 1936, when fire burned a fifth of the island and further reduced the browse supply, moose numbers had dropped to an estimated 400 to 500. From this low point, the herd increased again, aided by luxuriant resprouting on the burned area. By the later 1940s there were numerous signs that die-offs would again occur.

Catastrophic boom-and-bust cycles might have continued had it not been for the arrival, in the winter of 1948–49, of the gray wolf. Through the first half of the century its smaller cousin, the coyote, had been present; but coyotes seldom prey upon moose. By 1957, 15 to 25 wolves inhabited the island. Coyotes, probably killed off by the intolerant wolves, had disappeared. In 1960 David Mech, a Purdue graduate student studying wolves for a doctoral dissertation, determined after many hours of aerial observation that the wolves numbered 21 or possibly 22. This population was composed of a large pack of 15, which hunted mostly on the southwest two-thirds of the island, and small groups of two or three that hunted mostly on the northeast one-third and along the north shore.

From an aerial count made in March 1960, Mech estimated the moose herd at 600. He concluded that the wolves were controlling the herd at a level below that at which the food supply would control it, for browse species were growing in areas where they had not been evident for decades. Furthermore, the calculated annual kill of adults by wolves was nearly equal to the calculated number of yearlings surviving to join the breeding population each spring. And apparently the herd was healthy: the proportion of cows bearing twins as opposed to a single calf was much higher than it had been in the 1930s—a sign of good nutrition.

Research in the late 1960s and early 1970s indicated that the moose herd had increased, reaching a peak of about 1,500 in 1973. It then declined. Wolf numbers peaked at 50 in 1980 and then plummeted, reaching a worrisome low of 12 to 15 in the late 1980s and early 1990s. Meanwhile, the moose population rose again, up to about 2,400 in 1995.

It had become evident that a low- to medium-sized wolf population by itself would not stabilize the moose population, and that the ultimate determinant of moose numbers is the island's food supply. That supply depends on the stage of

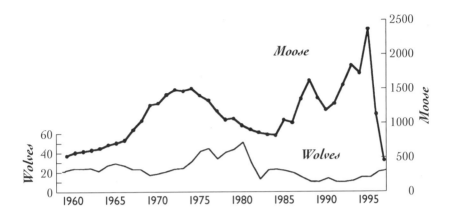

In the past four decades, moose on Isle Royale have declined dramatically twice, once from wolf predation and once from starvation. The recent period of exceptional growth and crash seems clearly linked to the wolf crash in 1980–82.

forest succession and the extent of browsing by moose. The relationship between these two factors is delicate and complex. In many parts of the northern forest, succession proceeds to a stable state in which spruce and fir form a closed canopy. In the course of this succession, food for moose declines as trees grow above browsing height and some favored browse species are shaded out. On Isle Royale, where moose densities are among the highest known and where wind takes a large toll of trees, succession seldom proceeds to a pure spruce-fir stand. The toppling of trees creates openings in which shrubs and saplings spring up, producing much browse. Browsing is so heavy in many of these areas that the young trees cannot grow up. This maintains a good food supply for a long time but eventually can result in elimination of the browse species and replacement by grass and unpalatable shrubs or by spruce. If it continues, such heavy browsing will cause certain tree species to drop out of the forest: mountain-ash essentially everywhere, aspen and cherry almost everywhere, paper birch and fir in many areas, and yellow birch in some areas. Only fire or a major decline in moose numbers will break this trend: major fires create so much new growth that moose cannot suppress it all; and a population decline has a similar effect. Thus the moose population cannot be expected to increase much more without the advent of fire.

Just as available browse limits moose numbers, available moose would ultimately limit wolf numbers. But there is considerable evidence that social pressures may set an upper limit to wolf density, even when the food supply goes on increasing. Within each pack there is a dominance order; each animal knows its social standing with respect to all the others. Furthermore, there are separate dominance orders among males and females. Normally, the lead, or alpha, male mates with the alpha female. Matings between subordinate animals are usually prevented by the lead pair. As a pack grows, sexual rivalries tend to become more and more complicated, and stress increases. Reproduction may also be inhibited by the dominance of large packs over smaller ones. If the territories of such packs are not well separated, the small pack probably has no chance of raising pups. Thus as wolf numbers grow in an area, increasing social controls apparently restrict reproduction.

Death of pups is another, perhaps greater, control on numbers. Many pups die during the denning period, from causes not yet well understood. Others succumb after leaving the den. If a pup survives its first six months—until fall—its chances of living several more years are good.

Additional controls on the Isle Royale wolf population have become apparent in recent years. Canine parvovirus, a virulent disease of dogs, probably arrived on Isle Royale in 1979–81, and is thought to have caused the high mortality of wolves that occurred from 1981 to 1988, at which time parvovirus seems to have disappeared from the island. The low reproductive rate in the late 1980s and early 1990s may have been due to inbreeding. Genetic testing of blood samples from captured wolves indicated that all the island's wolves were descended from a single female that arrived in the winter of 1948–49.

In 1994, eight pups survived to winter and the total population rose to 15. There were 17 wolves at the beginning of the 1995 winter study but only 15 at the end. The alpha female from the east pack killed the alpha female from the middle pack and then died herself. In the 1995–96 winter study the wolf population had increased to 22. Aging of the moose herd provided a growing supply of vulnerable moose, so everyone hoped this would lead to a recovery in the wolf population. If not, a major chapter in the story of Isle Royale may come to an end.

Among Isle Royale's other animals, there are examples of both stable and unstable populations. The red squirrel population, though high, does not change greatly. As we have seen, this species has no really efficient predator, like the marten, on the island. (Not yet, anyway. What may have been a marten was photographed in the summer of 1993.) The squirrel's numbers are regulated largely through reproductive control. Females bear only one litter, averaging three young, in a year, and many do not reproduce at all in poor cone years. Thus the birth rate is low, the survival rate is high, and the chatter of red squirrels remains perennially ubiquitous.

Deer mice, though without competition from other small mammals except red squirrels, remain rather thinly distributed over the island. In favorable habitat, there are only one or two per acre. This low density, which is comparable to that on the mainland, must represent the limit allowed by available food and shelter, and suggests that the island deer mice have not occupied the ecological niches of other small rodents found on the mainland but not on the island. Though deer mouse numbers in early spring may be only one-eighth of those in late August, numbers from one spring to another do not vary greatly.

On the other hand, snow-shoe hares are famous for their boom-and-bust population cycles. For instance, systematic observations of snowshoe hares on the island in 1993 revealed only about one twenty-fifth the number of those in 1988. Like rabbits, hares have a high reproductive potential, and variations

in the reproductive rate, influenced by availability of nutrients, seem the prime reason for fluctuations in the hare population. Diseases and predation are factors in the downward part of the cycle.

Genetic testing has shown that Isle Royale's wolf population may be descended from a single female that arrived in 1948–49.

Predators that depend on hares are forced to take the same population roller-coaster ride. On Isle Royale, red fox numbers might be expected to follow this pattern. Before 1970 they seemed to do so, but not in the years since. The fox population does seem to fluctuate widely, however, judging from aerial counts in winter. If the lynx, now rare or absent from the island, were established here, its population swings *could* be expected to parallel those of the hare. But the usually low hare populations here do not seem adequate to support lynxes permanently.

Insect populations, too, sometimes explode and then fade. The larch sawfly boomed early in this century, defoliated many larches (tamaracks), and then dwindled. The spruce budworm multiplied fast in the 1930s, causing concern for the firs, a chief winter food of moose, then also extremely abundant. But after that time the insect quietly retreated. Its levels, like those of most insects, continue to rise and fall. The outbreak of the large aspen tortrix in the 1970s gave another example of the normally temporary nature of such explosions. As with other animals, insect outbreaks are eventually controlled by food supply, predators, disease, parasites, and weather, and by aspects of the species' life history.

What determines the relative stability or instability of populations? This is a complex question with no simple answer, but an important part of it lies in the diversity of species present. The more species present in an area, the more stable its populations are likely to be. This is so because fluctuations within individual species tend to cancel each other out, and because various species act as a check on, or a food supply for, other species. If, for instance, Isle Royale had more species of small mammals, it probably could support more foxes, and more small mammals might reduce the swings in the fox population by providing more choice of food, and a more stable total supply, in the critical winter season. If, say, voles were on the island, their numbers might be high at a time when hares were scarce, thus allowing more foxes to survive the winter. If, on the other hand, wolves disappeared from the island, moose population fluctuations would probably be accentuated, as they were early in this century.

As a rule, islands have fewer species of animals than do mainland areas of comparable size and habitats. This is true mainly because for many species islands are difficult to reach. And if an established species is somehow wiped out, it may be a long time before new colonists arrive to try again. On the mainland, migration from one area to another is much easier. A number of species of vertebrates, as we have seen, and perhaps hundreds of invertebrates that live on the north shore of Lake Superior are not found on Isle Royale. Perhaps if all these were present, animal numbers on the island would be somewhat more stable.

However much or little they may fluctuate, the animal populations on Isle Royale are ultimately controlled by the quantity and quality of vegetation. This is so because green plants, directly in the case of herbivores and indirectly in the case of carnivores, supply virtually all the food for animals. Exactly which animal species and how many of each are present at any given time depend on the species available in the region, their particular food requirements, and a number of other factors, some of which we have just considered.

Isle Royale's green plants, in turn, depend on water — much of which comes from Lake Superior — carbon dioxide, and the energy of sunlight to produce the sugar from which the compounds necessary to sustain life are built. Plants also require mineral nutrients from the environment for their maintenance. So the potential amount of vegetation on Isle Royale is controlled by the amount of incoming energy from the sun, the amount of moisture, and the mineral nutrients in the soil and air. The nutrients further determine the type and quality of the vegetation as food for animals. In northern coniferous forests the water percolating down through the soil carries much of the needed nutrients below the reach of

A Researcher's Life ►● Much of what we know about animal life on Isle Royale comes from Rolf Peterson and his associates. Since 1970, Rolf has studied wolf-moose relationships and assisted with or directed studies on other animals of the island.

It's been an adventurous and rewarding life. ►● Rolf did his Ph.D. work under Durward Allen, the Purdue University professor who launched the Isle Royale wolf-moose studies in 1958. In 1975 Rolf took over direction of the studies and moved to Michigan Technological University in Houghton, where he is a professor of wildlife ecology in the School of Forestry. ►● The research has winter and summer phases. Each year from early January to mid-March, weather permitting, Rolf and his graduate students, assisted by park staff members who come out for two-week shifts, headquarter in cabins at Windigo. Besides directing the research, Rolf sets the bunkhouse rules and bakes the bread. Each good flying day, Rolf and pilot Don E. Glaser track wolf packs by air, flying in a small plane a few hundred feet above the treetops. This often involves circling down for a closer look, a maneuver that tends to flip your stomach. "Fortunately, I managed to get used to air sickness," Rolf says. "Some people never do." When moose kills have been located, Rolf and his assistants snowshoe back the next day to collect parts—sometimes 70 pounds worth—for analysis. Cross-sections of teeth show age of the moose, bones reveal any arthritis, and fat content of the bone marrow indicates the moose's nutritional condition. ►● Rolf's summer research focuses on further seeking and examining moose kills, aided by Earthwatch volunteers, trapping and radiocollaring wolves, and

tracking collared wolves from the ground and air. ➤● The work has special moments. Once in his graduate student days, a pack of wolves approached Rolf and his wife Carolyn to within 8 feet, a rare and privileged experience, since Isle Royale wolves almost always take great pains to avoid humans. And sometimes there are scares. On one winter flight, Rolf and the pilot were overtaken by a sudden snowstorm that seemed to come out of nowhere. "We could barely see," he recalled. To get back to Windigo, "we ended up following the shoreline just above tree level," flying along every little indentation of the shore. "Eventually we were able to make out our dock and make a safe landing." ➤●
Another time Rolf found himself out on the ice examining a dead moose calf with the mother approaching from shore. He took off running down the shore and climbed a tree "just as the mother moose reached the base of the tree.  She was only a few feet away, and we just stared at each other for what seemed like an eternity." Eventually she left, allowing the shaken Rolf to escape. In spring and fall, Rolf becomes Professor Peterson again, teaching, supervising students, writing, attending conferences, and pursuing that unpleasant necessity of research scientists—funds to continue the work. Now, too, he must confront the meaning of his data. What, finally, is the nature of the wolf-moose relationship? Can we understand and predict how the populations will interact and change? With all its surprises over the years, this relationship is still something of a mystery. That's what keeps Rolf Peterson and his students coming back year after year to this marvelous island laboratory. ➤●

Green plants, such as blueberry and bog rosemary, are the foundation of terrestrial food chains.

plant roots, and the low rates of evaporation do not allow a counterflow of minerals upward. This mineral deficiency, together with the lower amount of sunlight, results in less production of plant matter here than in the deciduous forests to the south and considerably less than in tropical forests. The island's forests are, however, much more productive than Arctic tundra, which suffers from greater deficiencies. Research by a Yale University team suggests that Isle Royale supports more animal life than do many other parts of the northern forest at similar latitudes. They suspect that this can be attributed to the island's underpinning of basalt and sedimentary rocks, which contribute more of the essential minerals to the soil than does the granite that underlies large areas elsewhere.

The relationships between incoming energy, minerals, surrounding water, plants, and animals can be studied particularly well on islands because the water prevents much interchange with the mainland. On Isle Royale, for instance, the interdependencies of moose, wolf, vegetation, and water are much easier to study than they are in mainland areas because here the animals are virtually penned in by Lake Superior: their numbers are not often affected by immigration or emigration. The added fact that nature is allowed to operate unhindered creates an outdoor ecological laboratory of exceptional value—one that has attracted scientists since the middle of the nineteenth century.

What does Isle Royale tell us about our own relationships with nature? One clear message is that we should encourage diversity. For instance, we create very unstable situations by devoting large areas to one crop, which can be devastated by a single insect species or disease. Such monocultures limit the animal life that can act as checks on exploding pest populations. And we never know when some obscure plant or animal may be needed to provide something required for our own welfare or that of our environment. But the fundamental message, which should have reached most people by now, is that we, like other animals, are ultimately controlled by our environment. If we do not stabilize our numbers, we face the unpleasant alternative of starvation, disease, and warfare. And if we continue to poison our environment, it will eventually poison us.

For the earth, too, is an island—an island in the sea of space. All that we have is here, finite, wrapped within our round shore.

The Guardians

*I*t takes a lot of work and caring to let Isle Royale be what nature wants it to be. With all the people coming here, and with the unfortunate by-products of our civilization also arriving by air and water, nature is hard put to keep things natural. It is the job of the National Park Service to help nature do that. It's also the job of researchers, long-time residents, park volunteers, and every visitor.

One way or another, all one hundred or so of the Isle Royale National Park staff are here to protect the park and to help visitors enjoy it. It's a highly seasonal job. As soon as the ice relinquishes its grip on the island, Park Service people start coming out to inspect and get things ready. Among the first, in late April, are the boatshop foreman and his assistant, chugging across the 70 miles of Lake Superior in the 20-foot *Tobin H.* to fire up the generators at Rock Harbor Lodge, Mott Island, and Windigo. At the same time, rangers come over in a 26-foot Bertram to check facilities all around the island, put in diving and navigational buoys, and make contact with any intrepid early visitors. Sometimes they have to break a little ice to get where they want to go, and some places, like McCargoe Cove, won't let them in until the ice goes out.

In early to mid-May, the rest of the staff, except for a few stationed at the visitor center in Houghton, comes out on the *Ranger III*. They are maintenance workers, administrators, resource managers, interpreters, and emergency services rangers. Each has a specific role in the overall mission.

The maintenance people go to work on trails and facilities, clearing, cleaning, repairing. Roving trail crews, backpacking with pulaskis, saws, and shovels, cover all 165 miles of park trails in three weeks to remove or cut the many windthrown trees. Living in tents, project trail crews start in on specific projects, such as rehabilitating a 10-mile section of a trail—clearing out water bars, repairing bridges, maybe rerouting a part of the trail to reduce erosion or avoid wet places—or repairing shelters and improving tent pads at campgrounds. Then there's that vital necessity of privy maintenance—cleaning them, digging new holes, moving privies. "There's always a dozen or so of the park's 70 privies that need moving," said long-time Trail and Campground Foreman Doug Boose in 1994.

Maintenance crews spend their first three weeks on the island clearing and repairing the park's 165 miles of trails.

With college training in forestry and recreation, Doug had learned about trails on the job, starting in 1974. "For this work, you need people who like to work hard. You carry the tools by hand. No bulldozers, no motel rooms." When it comes to building trails, "it's as much art as science," he said.

"You can read about it, but each situation is different, with different geology, soils, vegetation. You have to make your own decisions. When we route trails, we try to avoid flat and steep areas, maintain a 5 to 15 percent grade. Flat areas don't drain, and steep areas are hard walking and erosion prone. We want it to be pleasant. We try to use the terrain in artful ways, make the trail varied, not monotonous."

Student Conservation Association helpers and other volunteers pitch in to help the trail crews.

Volunteers and Student Conservation Association helpers pitch in with the trail crews. The SCA high school students come out for a month or so, working on specific projects like tent pad construction. Volunteers from the Sierra Club, American Hiking Society, and other groups have also come out for shorter periods.

Park management is based on laws, like a park's enabling legislation, on Park Service policies and regulations, and on knowledge about the park. The knowledge comes primarily from research, and it is the resource manager's job to identify the research needed, to see that it gets done, and to use the new knowledge in managing the park's resources.

The cultural resources

management specialist is concerned with such things as the future of abandoned structures such as fish houses at fishing camps and cottages whose owners' leases have expired. Should some be kept for their historical value or used as housing? Protection of underwater cultural resources such as old boats, shipwrecks, and relics at historic sites is another important responsibility. Such objects must be found and their significance understood—a job for researchers. A Park Service team provided this information for shipwrecks in admirable detail in the 1980s. In the 1990s a volunteer researcher documented the hand-crafted "vernacular" boats left by Isle Royale fishermen ashore or underwater, as part of continuing research on commercial fishing here. Further research on Indians, mining, logging, and trapping will expand knowledge of these activities and their effects on the island. All will build on older research, such as the intensive studies of mining and commercial fishing conducted by Lawrence Rakestraw in the 1960s.

Numerous natural resource issues confront the park as well. How do moose, wolves, other animals, and fire affect the vegetation of Isle Royale? What should the park service do if the wolf population approaches zero—import new wolves or let nature take its course? What is the natural fire regime here? What are the trends in the park's fish populations? Is air and water pollution having a significant effect on park resources?

Research on such questions comes under the purview of the natural resource management specialist. This position oversees the monitoring of various animal populations, such as beavers, eagles, ospreys, loons, and forest birds.

Fire is an important issue in national parks, and Isle Royale is no exception. Allowing lightning fires to burn, as long as they don't threaten human life or property, is one way the park's managers promote natural conditions on the island. Ninety-five percent of the park's land is zoned for this "prescribed natural fire." All human-caused fires, however, are put out. Because there was so much burning during the mining and logging eras, the natural fire regime is poorly understood. Is it frequent small fires, infrequent large fires, or what? The natural resource manager would like to know the answer.

The flora of virtually every national park includes some exotic, or nonnative, plants, and even the remoteness of Isle Royale has not protected it from this infection. Earlier inhabitants, birds, water, and wind brought such foreigners as dandelions and red and white clover. Some, like these, do not seem to threaten the native vegetation, and are ignored. But spotted knapweed is pulled up wherever found, since this one could become a problem. The park staff is always on the lookout for any exotic species—animals as well, like the Norway rat—that could endanger the native ecosystem.

Our current knowledge of Isle Royale's natural history is built on the work of a venerable line of researchers going back well before the establishment of the park. Several University of Michigan scientists working under the direction of Charles C. Adams conducted the island's first comprehensive ecological survey in 1904 and 1905. William S. Cooper carried out classic studies on plant succession here in 1909–1910. Around 1930 Adolph Murie, a famous early park service biologist, described the widespread impact of a very high moose population on the vegetation. Laurits Krefting, a U.S. Fish and Wildlife Service biologist, followed up with studies of moose-vegetation impacts and other wildlife investigations from the 1940s through the 1960s. Next we must

Boats ►● Of all the tools used to protect and study Isle Royale, none is more essential than boats. If you want to get somewhere or deliver something, you usually need a boat. This dependence on boats for transportation and sometimes one's very life makes boats seem almost living things, each with its own personality. They deserve tribute. ►● Like fishermen's Mackinaw sailing schooners, as they called them, and gas boats in the past, the park service boats are admirably designed for  their particular jobs. This Isle Royale "navy" consists of some 40 vessels, from the 165-foot *Ranger III* to speedy patrol and rescue Bertrams, tough, noisy Monarch workboats, down to 10-foot Zodiacs. Some of them are pictured here. ►●

honor the long-term studies of wolves and moose directed by Durward Allen and then Rolf Peterson. These began in 1958, with David Mech doing the pioneer research, and they still continue. Working during this same long span of years, Bob Janke has studied forest succession after fire and other botanical subjects. These are just a few of the well-known natural science researchers here; many others have also made important contributions. All have helped to preserve Isle Royale and guide its management through the understanding they have achieved.

Some questions have both natural and cultural elements. One that looms very large concerns locations and numbers of visitors. How many should be allowed at specific locations, and how many should be allowed on the island at one time or during a season? Too many people can have unacceptable physical impacts and can diminish the sense of solitude and wilderness. And people's concepts of wilderness vary. One person may think an hour's walk from Rock Harbor Lodge is a wilderness experience, while another may be unhappy if he sees another person during two weeks in the backcountry. Both natural and social scientists will have to look into these issues.

Research information is also the basis for the park's education and interpretive program, which informs visitors, enhances their appreciation of Isle Royale, and builds support for protecting it. The chief naturalist oversees this program—a diverse mix of walks, talks, exhibits, nature trails, and other channels of communication.

The chief naturalist's season begins with selecting seasonal interpreters and then, in early June when they arrive, training them. This is an intensive process, especially for the new ones, who must learn about the park and prepare pro-

grams in two short weeks, along with learning about boat operation and park procedures. The interpreters, including volunteers as well as seasonal and perma-

Visitors to Isle Royale gain valuable insight to the park's salient features through interpretive guided walks.

nent employees, talk about the park's salient features of natural and cultural history, but they also focus their programs on various resource management issues—things visitors should know about since they are among the owners of Isle Royale National Park.

Two other parts of the program take different, rather unusual approaches to interpretation. Down at the Edisen Fishery, a site in Rock Harbor named after Pete Edisen, a longtime commercial fisherman there, Les Mattson and his wife Donna in the mid-1990s were showing visitors around the fish house, with all its fishing gear, and describing the commercial fisherman's life. Mattson, formerly a full-time fisherman at Munising, Michigan, continued a small-scale operation here for interpretive purposes, setting a few nets around Middle Islands Passage and Rock Harbor and selling the lake trout and whitefish to the Rock Harbor Lodge. Commercial fishing was an important part of Isle Royale's cultural history, and the park administrators want to keep that memory alive.

Each summer, a cottage out at Scoville Point is home to a succession of four to six artists-in-residence. These artists paint, sketch, photograph, or write about Isle Royale and give talks to visitors about their work and their unique vision of the park—yet another form of interpretation.

Many people keep a long-term bond with Isle Royale, and among these is the park's first chief naturalist—Bob Linn. Bob first came here in 1947, bringing Explorer Scouts on a camping trip. His career with the National Park Service began in 1952 with a job at Isle Royale. His first assistants in interpretation in 1955 were Bob Janke—who became a professor at Michigan Technological University and a perennial student of Isle Royale's forests—and Bob Johnsson, who later directed an exhibits division in the Park Service's Harpers Ferry Center. Bob Linn wrote a Ph.D. dissertation about the forests of Isle Royale and later became chief scientist of the National Park Service. Still he returned to Isle Royale whenever he could. He eventually moved back to the Houghton-Hancock area to oversee research conducted for the park service at Michigan Technological University and remained in Hancock when he retired. He founded the Isle Royale Natural History Association and has served on its board. To help me in revising this book, he took me to various parts of the island in his boat. I imagine he will come here, and work for the good of Isle Royale, as long as he can move and think.

In Isle Royale's administrative scheme, the chief ranger has responsibility for natural and cultural resource management, interpretation, law enforcement, emergency services, and concessions. The law enforcement rangers, stationed at several places around the island, do much more than enforce laws, perhaps the least enjoyable part of their job. They look after the well-being of visitors, answer questions, and, if need be, enforce the park regulations. These regulations are designed to ensure visitors' safety and protect park resources. Park rangers are frequently called on to do other things, such as conduct interpretive programs, clear trails, and rescue injured visitors. In a relatively small park like Isle Royale, everybody pitches in to get the job done, whether it is in their job description or not. "A Ranger's Life" presents a picture of one such ranger's experience.

The ultimate responsibility for Isle Royale National Park and its health lies with the superintendent. One of the superintendent's chief concerns here, as in many parks, is how to balance preservation and use. Listen to a superintendent of the 1990s, Doug Barnard: "With the improvements in boats, the park has become more accessible, and with more leisure time now and probably in the future I expect increasing visitation. This year through August we're up 13½ percent. Sometimes boaters are rafted up four to six deep at docks. But this is a fragile environment because it's so cold, and mostly rock and water. Clean air, clean water—and many people say solitude—are our greatest resources. It's difficult to protect these things with increasing numbers of people in the confines of an island.

"Our enabling legislation in 1931 directed us to keep the park in primeval condition. The Wilderness Act and designation in 1976 of 99 percent of the park as wilderness require

A Ranger's Life ➤ After 13 years, Elen Maurer knew something about Isle Royale. Like many park rangers, Elen began as a seasonal. She operated the Feldtmann Fire Tower in the southwestern part of the island. "It was a fabulous introduction to the National Park Service," she said. "My main responsibility was talking to the visitors who stopped by the tower." Two more summers as a seasonal interpreter at Rock Harbor and Windigo broadened her experience. During another summer, at Apostle Islands National Lakeshore in Wisconsin, she received training in law enforcement and boat handling. With these skills, plus experience as a diver, she was selected to be a "permanent, subject to furlough" at Isle Royale. That meant she, like many others on the staff, had a job half of the year but was off in the winter. ➤ For the next nine years she settled in as North Shore Ranger at Amygdaloid Island, an elongated strip of rock and forest buffering the coves and harbors at the northeast end of Isle Royale from the waves of Lake Superior. Here she watched over visitors to that area, giving information, leading a weekly walk to the Minong copper mine, helping in emergencies, and making sure visitors followed safety and resource protection regulations. "There's very little human crime here," she said. "We have a high-caliber visitor out here. Most of the violations are resource violations." As the dive team leader, she helped put up and take out diving and navigational buoys, recovered lost items, inspected docks, checked on underwater cultural resources, and occasionally had to assist at the scene of an accident. ➤ "People are pretty careful here," knowing they're a long way from any hospital or other source of specialized help, but people do get in trouble. Sometimes hikers are injured or become ill. "I've had a few carryouts," Elen said. "That's mostly sweat and grunt work." And boats get lost in fog or become disabled. One large sailboat lost power out beyond Passage Island and couldn't make it back to Isle Royale against the strong wind. "We went out in a 31-foot twin diesel Bertram to tow her in. It was hard to get close in the 6 or 7-foot waves," but they managed to tie up and bring the boat to Tobin Harbor. ➤● It's not just the regular work that she liked. "I love watching the seasons here, the northern lights, paddling along the shore in my kayak, fishing or just enjoying … being close to moose. One summer I helped Rolf Peterson trap wolves for radiocollaring. It was a rare privilege to touch a wild wolf." The human associations were a big part of it, too, getting to know "the people who care about this place, who raised families out here," and having the bond with park service people who keep coming back. ➤● In 1994 Elen was the acting West District Ranger at Windigo, with added, supervisory responsibilities. With her husband Joel (Buzz) Brown, a trail crew boat operator, she looked forward to ever-widening experiences on Isle Royale. ➤●

that these lands retain their primeval character, 'without permanent improvements or human habitation.' Furthermore, the park's designation as an International Biosphere Reserve in 1980 emphasized its importance and gave us additional responsibility for research. We need to go through the General Management Plan process as soon as possible, and I think one result of that will be a reservation system within the next 10 years."

The park season on Isle Royale winds down in October. The trail crews lean the picnic tables up against trees. Boats are hauled out of the water, some to be painted and stored. During the month, most of the park staff boards the *Ranger III* to return to the mainland. Early in November the few remaining close things up. The boatshop foreman shuts off the generators and rangers patrol for any last visitors. The island is now deserted for the winter, except for the two-month wolf studies. Back in Houghton, the staff operates the visitor center, works with schools, and begins preparations for the next season on Isle Royale.

As we have seen, the park staff is supported in its work by researchers, volunteers, and on occasion by a host of organizations. Constantly at work is the Isle Royale Natural History Association, which sells publications and other items about the park to support park interpretation and other activities. Now, in these times of tight park budgets, the park is looking increasingly at partnerships with the private sector to raise money for needed projects and facilities.

You and I, whether as visitors or simply as public owners of Isle Royale, are also asked to be guardians. As visitors we must tread lightly on the lands and waters, and as owners we should support all efforts to protect this fragile wilderness. It is worth the work.

Isle Royale: A Wilderness Park ►◄ Since the late 1800s, many people have been attracted to Isle Royale solely for its remote, wilderness qualities, and that theme has resounded through all subsequent discussions of the island's ownership and management. ►◄ National park status gave strong protection to Isle Royale's wilderness character, but it was the Wilderness Act of 1964 that provided for congressional designation of areas within federal public land as "wilderness" and specifically restricted their use and management so as to protect that quality. The act was a response to the intensifying use of public land in America and to the widespread desire to preserve the opportunity for wilderness experience. It defines wilderness as "an area where the earth and its community of life are untrammeled by man, where man himself is a visitor who does not remain" and

which, among other characteristics, "has outstanding opportunities for solitude or a primitive and unconfined type of recreation." In 1976 Congress designated 131,888 acres of Isle Royale National Park as  wilderness and 231 acres as potential wilderness addition. With a slight subsequent increase, the park's wilderness now constitutes 99 percent of the land area, excluding only a few developed or historical areas. ►◄ Visitors to Isle Royale need to understand what wilderness is and to do their part in protecting it. This means caring for the land and water, and respecting the desire and right of others for solitude and quiet. With the present popularity of Isle Royale among backpackers, canoeists, kayakers, and boaters, it will take the special efforts of each person to preserve that fragile quality called wilderness. ►◄

Isle Royale
AN INTERNATIONAL
BIOSPHERE RESERVE

*T*he values and potential of Isle Royale National Park extend well beyond its protection of the wild island ecosystem and the enjoyment the park gives visitors. Those extended values were recognized in 1980 when the park was designated an International Biosphere Reserve.

Biosphere reserves are a key element of the Man and the Biosphere Program, which was launched by the United Nations Educational, Scientific, and Cultural Organization in 1971 to provide international cooperation in learning how to address the environmental problems that beset societies around the world. Biosphere reserves are centers for research and education toward this end. They are also examples of characteristic ecosystems of the world where conservation of those natural systems and their genetic resources can be assured.

Both protected and experimental areas are included in most biosphere reserves in order to learn the best ways of using various environments while still maintaining their biological diversity and ecological stability. In the United States, many biosphere reserves consist of two or more units, such as a national park and an experimental forest, to achieve the varied purposes. The national park serves as an undisturbed control area for comparison with the manipulated experimental area. What is learned can be applied elsewhere in the region and often in similar environments in other parts of the world.

Isle Royale was selected as an outstanding example of southern boreal forest. At this writing it has not been officially joined as a biosphere reserve with other areas in the Lake Superior region, but it does cooperate with other areas in addressing regional environmental issues. Isle Royale is involved in the Lake Superior Binational Program and cooperates with the other Lake Superior national park sites—Apostle Islands National Lakeshore, Pictured Rocks National Lakeshore, Grand Portage National Monument, Keweenaw National Historical Park, and Canada's Pukaskwa National Park—in an education program on the Superior Basin for area students and residents. Much of the research on Isle Royale, such as studies of atmospheric inputs and global change research, serves regional, national, and international needs as well as those of park management.

In its role as a biosphere reserve, the park is much more than an island. It is a piece of the world.

Departure

All too soon our visit ends. We must board the boat or plane and return to our mainland life. But though we leave the island, the island does not leave us. For we carry away memories: of a bull moose feeding in an evening lake, of fog rising from a wild rock shore, of night talk around a warm fire. And perhaps we try to put it all together—to see what the island has meant to us.

For some, it has meant a chance to cruise a wild shore, simply enjoying it or pursuing large, wild fish. For others, the scientist particularly, the island has meant an opportunity to study nature in a place where humans intrude but little and isolation produces a unique natural laboratory, a nearly closed system.

For most people, the island has meant a brief experience of wilderness—a glimpse of the primordial world and of oneself as a human animal in it. The wilderness value of Isle Royale calls, I think, for more discussion, because it is a fragile thing requiring careful protection. More than to any other national park, people go to Isle Royale primarily for a wilderness experience. Yet, embracing 200 square miles of land and water, it is a small place as national parks go. As more people come to enjoy its wilderness, each person's wilderness experience is diminished, since solitude is its central ingredient. Clearly, there are limits beyond which visitation must not go. What those limits should be, how they should be achieved, and how much freedom visitors should be allowed once they get to the park are questions the park service wrestles with and with which all Americans—the owners of Isle Royale—should be concerned. In both a psychological and an ecological sense, Isle Royale has a limited carrying capacity for people as well as for wildlife.

Another important part of the Isle Royale experience is the opportunity it gives us to be truly human. In this basic situation, we learn again the simple joys of eating after hunger, getting warm after being cold, drying out after getting soaked, or resting after a long day's hike. And we learn again the value of the individual. With pressures removed, fewer people around, and a dependence on those few in case of emergency, we recognize our need for each other and have the chance to know each other simply as unique human beings. The common experience of all these things creates a special fellowship.

Finally, living on Isle Royale even briefly gives us a rare chance to gain perspective on ourselves and our civilization. Somehow the remoteness and the difference of this place wipe out our old images and allow new ones to form against the simple, natural background around us.

And so we return to our man-made world, shocked by its concrete and cars, but knowing that the island remains—a contrast, a restorer, a measure of our civilization.

Suggested Reading

Allen, Durward. 1993 (revised edition). *Wolves of Minong: Isle Royale's Wild Community.* The University of Michigan Press, Ann Arbor.

Du Fresne, Jim. 1991 (2nd edition). *Isle Royale National Park: Foot Trails and Water Routes.* The Mountaineers, Seattle, Washington.

Gale, Thomas P., and Kendra L. Gale. 1995. *Isle Royale: A Photographic History.* Isle Royale Natural History Association, Houghton, Michigan.

Glime, Janice M. 1993. *The Elfin World of Mosses and Liverworts of Michigan's Upper Peninsula and Isle Royale.* Isle Royale Natural History Association, Houghton, Michigan.

Huber, N. King. 1983 (revised edition). *The Geologic Story of Isle Royale National Park.* Avery Color Studios, Marquette, for Isle Royale Natural History Association, Houghton, Michigan.

Isle Royale Natural History Association. 1994 (and updates as available). *Isle Royale National Park Checklist of Birds.* Houghton, Michigan.

Isle Royale Natural History Association. 1995 (and updates as available). *Isle Royale National Park Checklist of Mammals.* Houghton, Michigan.

Janke, Robert. 1996 (revised 2nd edition). *The Wildflowers of Isle Royale.* Isle Royale Natural History Association, Houghton, Michigan.

Lagler, Karl F., and Charles R. Goldman. 1982 (2nd revised edition). *Fishes of Isle Royale.* Isle Royale Natural History Association, Houghton, Michigan.

Lenihan, Daniel J. 1994. *Shipwrecks of Isle Royale National Park*. Lake Superior Port Cities, Duluth, Minnesota.

McIntyre, Judith. 1988. *The Common Loon: Spirit of Northern Lakes*. University of Minnesota Press, Minneapolis.

Peterson, Rolf O. 1995. *The Wolves of Isle Royale: A Broken Balance*. Willow Creek Press, Minocqua, Wisconsin.

Rennicke, Jeff. 1989. *Isle Royale: Moods, Magic, & Mystique*. Isle Royale Natural History Association, Houghton, Michigan.

Sivertson, Howard. 1992. *Once Upon An Isle: The Story of Fishing Families on Isle Royale*. Wisconsin Folk Museum, Mount Horeb, Wisconsin.

Slavick, Allison, and Robert Janke. 1993 (3rd edition). *The Vascular Flora of Isle Royale National Park*. Isle Royale Natural History Association, Houghton, Michigan.

Weber, Bruce (editor). 1992. *Borealis: An Isle Royale Potpourri*. Isle Royale Natural History Association, Houghton, Michigan.

These books, and others on Isle Royale, may be obtained from the Isle Royale Natural History Association, 800 East Lakeshore Drive, Houghton, Michigan 49931-1895; telephone 1-800-678-6925.